WOMEN
ARE THE
FUTURE OF
ISLAM

SHERIN
KHANKAN

WOMEN
ARE THE
FUTURE OF
ISLAM

A memoir
of hope

RIDER

LONDON • SYDNEY • AUCKLAND • JOHANNESBURG

1 3 5 7 9 10 8 6 4 2

Rider, an imprint of Ebury Publishing,
20 Vauxhall Bridge Road,
London SW1V 2SA

Rider is part of the Penguin Random House group of companies whose
addresses can be found at global.penguinrandomhouse.com

Penguin
Random House
UK

First published in France as *La Femme est L'avenir de L'Islam* in 2017
First published in Great Britain by Rider in 2018

www.penguin.co.uk

A CIP catalogue record for this book is available from the British Library

ISBN 9781846045875

Typeset in 12/18 pt Garamond MT Std
by Integra Software Services Pvt. Ltd, Pondicherry

Printed and bound in Great Britain by Clays LTD, St Ives PLC

Penguin Random House is committed to a sustainable future for our
business, our readers and our planet. This book is made from
Forest Stewardship Council® certified paper.

*I pray for family stability (earth), emotional clarity (water) and the
courage to transform (fire) and burn up that which no longer serves love,
in order that something new can grow and find a higher perspective (air).*

*To my four children, my teachers: may you find balance
Aisha (air), Salaheddin (water), Djibril (fire) and Halima (earth).*

*And to the future generation of young Muslims, the secure, the homeless
and the refugees.*

To the loud and silent revolutions, the open and the hidden.

Contents

Introduction

I find it important to transform knowledge into activism. As a sociologist of religion and philosophy, and a practising Muslim, I can offer new perspectives on Islam in the West. This book is written from an activist's point of view and should be read as the individual story of a female Muslim activist in Europe. It is about my personal journey leading up to the establishment of the first mosque in Scandinavia with female imams and is for everyone who has an interest in Islam in the West and Islamic feminism. It does not represent a definitive text or absolutist view of Islam in Europe. I have found my place in the loneliness that comes from not being a member of the 'established consensus'.

It is my hope that this book can challenge patriarchal structures and readings of Islam, and the spread of Islamophobia, give new insight into contemporary female Islamic activism in the West and above all inspire a new generation of Muslim women to become activists and open up new mosques with female imams in other places around the world.

CHAPTER ONE

The making of Mariam Mosque

People go on claiming that something is impossible until someone comes along and just does it.

Halima Krausen, Muslim theologian and imam in
Hamburg, Germany

At the wheel of a borrowed car, Saliha and I head towards Copenhagen with the certainty that we are driving into history. In less than three hours, on this Friday, 26 August 2016, we will officially become the first female imams in Scandinavia. The title 'imam' is among the most notorious and disliked in Denmark due to the growing Islamophobia in the world. Saliha, a Danish convert and Arabic expert with a master's degree in Middle Eastern studies, and I have discussed the meaning of 'imam' many times since we first met and started our feminist movement. It is a controversial title, one that, to this day in Scandinavia and most places in the world, belongs exclusively to men. As we drive into the city centre, we play with words and both realise that, within an hour, 'imam' will transform into an 'imamah'. Saliha rejects the title 'imamah' for herself and prefers the term 'khatibah' (a woman who delivers the sermon). I hesitate as well. But in that very moment, realising that I am about to lead the Friday prayer, I decide to embrace the title of imamah with more confidence than ever before. It is a title that conveys a variety of meanings and practices, and can be defined as 'one who leads prayer', 'one who leads the mosque' or 'one who offers Islamic spiritual care'.

Now things are becoming real. Soon, when I recite the call to prayer, the first mosque for women in Scandinavia will be officially established. To be sure, it's an important event for Denmark, my native country, which consists of an archipelago and a peninsula tied to Germany that rises up like a ship's mast between the North Sea and the Baltic Sea. For six months, the opening of Mariam Mosque has been the subject of much discussion. However, we decided from the beginning to keep a low profile. In order to preserve the spiritual atmosphere, no media personnel were allowed inside the mosque. Only a few select female journalists, including a reporter from the *Guardian*, were allowed to participate in the prayer rituals, and then without cameras. The journalist from the *Guardian* then published an article online based on her experience. Little did we know that, soon afterwards, news of our mosque would spread worldwide, from Copenhagen to China. On the verge of becoming a female imam, my life is at a turning point.

* * *

Last night was a short one. Yesterday evening, all the members of the Femimam group, including me, were working at the mosque late into the night in order to have it ready for the opening. These things are always last minute. Saliha and I were on the late-night news. When we got back late to my seventeenth-century house in the countryside of Dragør, a historic fishing town over nine miles from the capital, neither of us could get to sleep until three in the morning. It's a good thing adrenaline cancels out fatigue, because as we drive towards Copenhagen and the rural landscape gives way to the first brick buildings of the suburbs, I recite the *adhan*, the lyrical call to prayer that penetrates the hearts of every Muslim to the point of becoming part of his or her being. I also recall the main points of my welcoming speech.

And suddenly we're in the city centre, driving along the canals, right by Borgen, the seat of the Danish parliament, known around the world from the eponymous television series. Mariam Mosque (named in homage to Mariam or Mary, the mother of religions, who 'unites and protects where there is no hope or light', has a sura, or chapter, of the Quran named after her, and is viewed by some Muslims as a female prophetic figure) is not far from here, at the heart of the touristy area, along a commercial pedestrian street where all the big fashion brands have stores: H&M, Malene Birger, Tiger of Sweden, etc. From the road, you wouldn't notice anything: the prayer room is on the first floor above street level, in a discreet building above a fast-food restaurant.

Denmark has two main mosques, both located outside the centre of Copenhagen, and equipped with minarets. In general, mosques are places of religious worship, but also education and some have even inspired humanitarian work and reforms. Opened in 2014, the big Hamad Bin Khalifa Mosque, financed by Qatar, is attended by Sunni Muslims. Imam Ali Mosque, which opened the following year and has a pretty blue dome, is the sacred house of worship for Shi'ite believers. The rest of the Danish Muslim community, over 270,000 strong (4.8 per cent of the total population of 5.6 million) meets in modest prayer rooms, most often in apartments or in the basements of buildings in peripheral areas. Mariam Mosque, which is open to all Muslims including Sunnis, Shi'ites, Alawis, Ahmadis and whoever else wants to come, is an all-inclusive mosque, based on Sufism, a mystical tradition and spiritual path within Islam.

Ideally placed in the town centre, the mosque is an apartment of just over 800 square feet, composed of a vast room adjoining a large prayer hall (forty feet long), an IKEA kitchen and four offices, all decorated with Scandinavian furniture and thick white carpet on the floors, accented with Iranian handmade carpets in the prayer hall. Our mosque also has a library with Islamic books donated by a publishing house. Not long ago, it was occupied by the consulate of a

Mediterranean member country of the European Union. But as soon as the diplomats gave notice, the owner, who knew I was looking for a place, offered the use of it to me in order to set up Mariam Mosque. Jacob Holdt, a world-famous photographer, especially renowned for his documentary work on the homeless in America, with whom he lived for seven years in the 1970s, is not a Muslim. He has simply spent his life embracing the cause of discriminated minorities (junkies, prostitutes, African-Americans, etc.). His method is to befriend his opponent through understanding the life stories of the other. I have been friends with Jacob for the last fifteen years, after he took an interest in our cause to promote Muslim feminism and the fight against Islamophobia. He, too, is exasperated by the racist, anti-Muslim climate spreading throughout Denmark, Europe and the world. He wanted to help us. *Allahu Akbar*, God is great.

Around noon, Mariam Mosque starts filling up. Dozens of women, with and without veils, flow in. The majority are practising Muslims, young women originating from Iran, Iraq, Palestine, Turkey and several African countries, but also converted Danes. There are non-Muslim women as well, including the invited journalist from the *Guardian*, some students, two Protestant pastors and a few representatives from secular feminist non-governmental organisations (NGOs) like KVINFO, the Danish Centre for Research on Women and Gender.

The excitement is palpable – this Friday is not like any other. Women greet and hug each other, volunteers serve coffee and tea along with homemade cakes and Syrian dishes like hummus and mutabbal (a dip made from aubergines and tahini) made by my father. I see new faces and faces I know. There is an atmosphere of trust and expectation in the build up to this long-awaited moment.

I slip away to the prayer room in order to focus before the *adhan* and prayer. As I start the first verses of the call to prayer (Allah is the greatest / I acknowledge that there is no God but Allah / I acknowledge that Muhammad is the Messenger of Allah / Come to prayer / Come to worship), I think of my Syrian grandfather, Naïm, a muezzin at the Great Mosque of Damascus (also known as the Umayyad Mosque), and my maternal grandparents who were farmers in Finland not far from the Arctic Circle, especially my grandfather Olavi, who fought in the Winter War of 1939–1940.[1] How surprised they would be to see their granddaughter wearing a hijab and calling believers to worship Allah! It's no small thing for the *adhan* to be performed by a woman. At Mariam Mosque, believers are delighted with women's sonorous voices, which they claim to find 'more soothing' than the typical masculine scansion. I agree: I, too, am moved by women's voices.

The room has filled up. There are around seventy participants, a third of whom are non-Muslim. Everyone appears at ease, appreciating the minimal yet warm decor: off-white curtains, lit chandeliers hanging at regular intervals and, on the qibla wall (which believers will face to pray), are verses from the Quran painted in calligraphy: 'I have created you male and female and made you into nations and tribes so that you may know each other ...'

When I finish singing the *adhan*, I begin my speech. I reveal the reason we started our mosque, which can be summed up in three ideas: offering and promoting a spiritual approach to Islam, based on a rereading of the Quran anchored in the reality of today's world, with a specific focus on women's rights; challenging patriarchal structures within religious and educational institutions, as well as patriarchal readings of the Quran and the Hadiths (the oral accounts written down after the Prophet's death that relate his words and actions); and promoting Islamic feminism in order to fight Islamophobia, which has escalated considerably since recent terrorist attacks in Paris and London. 'We are here to worship Allah,' I say, 'but also to challenge the conservatism and paternalism that reign supreme at the heart of our society where men have all the power. Too often, the younger generations desiring to fully live out their faith do not see themselves in these imams who come to us from within our own countries and abroad. We must offer alternatives.' I then describe my function as an imam: 'It's not just the person who leads prayer; the imam must be a spiritual guide, someone capable of answering the questions of our time. I'm a sociologist of religion and philosophy with specialisation in Islam, Sufism and Islamic activism. I took courses in Arabic and Islamic spiritual care and am currently in my fourth year towards becoming a certified psychotherapist. There are so many delicate subjects that women would rather discuss with other women than with men, starting with marriage difficulties. It's a well-known fact that imams in some traditional mosques aren't particularly receptive to certain problems women can have, such as psychological or physical violence ... '

Calmly and without raising my voice, I insist on the following: 'We are here to transform Islam in Europe and beyond, in order to show the world that this is a peaceful religion. We will change things from within. And we will take as long as necessary and go as far as China if we have to in repeating this message in order to put an end to the reign of ignorance.'

I don't forget to point out that, with the exception of the Friday prayer service, the mosque is open to men. There are actually some men who come during the week, often as part of a couple for marriage preparations or conversion, as well as for seminars, *dhikr* (Islamic mediation) devotions or lectures. In fact, the Islamic marriage contracts we offer are very different from those in other mosques around the world. Ours stipulate in the preamble that women have the right to divorce, polygamy is not an option and that, in the case of divorce, the woman keeps the same rights as the man and custody of the children is shared. In cases of physical violence or emotional abuse, the union is no longer valid. Moreover, at Mariam Mosque, we celebrate interfaith marriages because we acknowledge the reality that in Europe there is a high chance that a Muslim woman could fall in love with a non-Muslim man. We have to respond to this consideration and we do it by respecting Quranic legality, since you only need to study the sacred book to discover that it doesn't oppose such unions. I once officiated at the wedding of a Norwegian couple who had been refused by ninety-six different imams around the world. I'll come back to this point later in my story.

I give the floor to Saliha Marie Fetteh, who delivers the *khutbah*, or sermon. A Danish intellectual and author who converted to Islam many years ago, she is one of the khatibahs (women who give the sermons) of our mosque. In 2015, she joined the Femimam movement. I met her on 10 November of the previous year at Copenhagen airport. We were both heading to Istanbul along with other leading male imams from the area, where we were to participate in a conference on interfaith dialogue. An expert in Arabic, she lived in Iraq for eight years and now teaches college courses in Arabic, which she has mastered to perfection.

In order to block any criticism, to carry out our work without questions and assert our legitimacy, it is essential that the women who are actively involved at Mariam Mosque have solid and rigorous intellectual training. This is the case for Saliha Marie, but also for the three other women who are in the process of becoming female leaders on the team, who are all working to become female imams or khatibahs as well. Together, we hold advanced degrees in religion, Middle Eastern studies, the Arabic language, Islamic archeology and other related fields. My dream is to educate a new generation of the best-trained female imams in Islamic spiritual care in Denmark and Scandinavia. This discourages eventual charges of amateurism that some might wish to bring against us ...

Saliha's sermon is on the theme of 'women and Islam in the modern world'. In passing, she even amuses the assembly by bringing up 'the burkini controversy', a recent dispute which stirred up France, provoking a lack of understanding. 'I hope you're not looking for a burkini,' she says, 'because they've run out of stock all across Europe ever since the mayors in the French villages made them front-page news!' According to some sources, thousands of women ran out to buy burkinis in order to show their solidarity with Muslim women who chose to wear the Islamic swimsuits that were banned from certain beaches on France's Côte d'Azur.[2]

The moment for prayer has come. I invite the non-Muslims who are present to join in, and they agree. We lean over, get down on our knees, touch the ground with our foreheads, say 'Allahu Akbar', or 'Allah is great', and repeat it many times. For me, the act of sharing the experience with non-believers is nothing unusual – it is at the centre of my life, since I am the product of a marriage between a Finnish immigrant mother who attended a Protestant church and a Syrian father who barely practised his faith (though he's started praying five times a day again in recent years, ever since war broke out in his home country in 2011). As the ceremony finishes, I address the non-Muslims: 'And there you go, it's done: now you are all Muslims! Because according to Islamic tradition, your participation in this prayer means conversion. You knew that, right?' The assembly is a tiny bit dumbstruck but realises two seconds later that I'm joking. And everyone laughs.

There is a rare feeling of solidarity and unity in the room. Everything has gone marvellously and I'm incredibly happy about it. We've demonstrated that Christians and Muslims can pray together, side by side. Our 'direct action' is proof.

Curiously, the emotion that fills me is analogous and just as powerful as that which I feel listening to the *Kindertotenlieder* ('Songs on the Death of Children') by Gustav Mahler: an overwhelming emotion that brings us back to God. I'm not the only one who's moved – a woman I don't know looks like she's about to cry. She confesses to me that she's crying for the first time since her child died – somehow the prayer became a channel for her repressed sorrow, and the connection between the prayer and the Mahler song cycle I was thinking of, along with this grieving mother, shakes me. She assures me that she'll be back again. I then approach another woman, half Danish and half Arabic, who says she has always been the one to recite the Quran in her family. She holds a master's degree in Islamic archeology and she, too, has longed for a community that supports female leadership in the mosque. I ask her if she would consider joining our community by leading the next Friday prayer at Mariam Mosque, and she gladly accepts after some consideration. Ever since, she has been the main person who leads the Friday prayers for believers praying to Allah, because she is the most excellent out of all of us at reciting the Quran, while I usually deliver the *khutbah*.

A dynamic is triggered. In the media, the reception is positive, even if, as I expected, we experience criticism from just as many Muslim conservatives as from the Danish far right. The first group opposes us with arguments that are hardly surprising and are almost identical to those raised when the first female pastors were ordained in the Danish Lutheran Church in 1948: 'You're too sensitive, there are rules that apply to you, so you can't lead prayer … '; to which they add a special reason: 'Should we open a mosque reserved exclusively for men? Surely the Danish public would think it was an outrage.' On the opposite end, the Islamophobic Danish far right sees our initiative as another sign of the threat of Islam to 'Danish values'.

The women at Mariam Mosque are offering the world a counter-story, another narrative. For fifteen years, Islamic terrorism and the fear of it – from the Muhammad cartoons controversy, the shootings in Copenhagen in 2015, the Paris attacks the same year, not forgetting all the other attacks perpetrated by Muslim fanatics, especially in Iraq – have monopolised the public's attention, fanned Islamophobia, fed defiance and created fear within an entire community of believers, who are suddenly being called to justify actions that the public – need I say more? – clearly disapprove of and condemn. This prayer on Friday, 26 August 2016, belongs to a manifesto: it proclaims (or, rather, recalls) the existence of a contemporary, progressive, tolerant, peaceful, open and welcoming Islam. The one recognised by the silent majority, who practise this religion of peace and love daily.

Before becoming an imam, I was involved in politics in the Radikale Venstre (Danish Social Liberal Party), founded the Forum For Kritiske Muslimer (Forum for Critical Muslims, devoted to promoting debate in the Muslim community) and created an organisation to help girls and women subjected to psychological violence called Exitcirklen (the Exit Circle). On this Friday in August, upon returning home at the end of the afternoon, I think of my mother who, when I was little, affectionately called me Hyttynen ('mosquito') because 'I was very thin and always on the run'. Just after leading this first Friday prayer, my sister Nathalie calls me 'fierce and fearless', and my very close friends call me 'the tigress'. My father always told me – and still does: 'Just put your feet down, child. You're going too fast, and no one can follow you. Put things on hold and just breathe.'

When I enter the house, I find the other 'wild animals': my four children, Aisha, Salaheddin, Djibril and Halima Mariam, aged thirteen, nine, eight and six. They belong to the four elements – air, water, fire and earth – and are as unruly one expects children to be. One day, around the time of the opening of Mariam Mosque, I was getting ready for the Friday prayer, putting on my white scarf and Syrian *galabiyya* (a long-sleeved garment that goes all the way down to the ankles), a gift from my father that I converted into my imamah dress. Halima Mariam, my youngest, had a friend over. Halima's friend whispered in her ear: 'Do you know what an imam is?'

Halima looked at her with proud tigress eyes and answered, 'Yes, it's a woman who does very important things!'

This story shows that it's possible to change a century of fixed narrative in the mind of a five-year-old (Halima's age at the time).

Six months after the opening of Mariam Mosque, I take my four children to visit it on a day of prayer. I write notes to each of their teachers to justify their absence. 'On Friday my children will be off school since I will be showing them the school of real life and introduce them to Islamic feminism in practice', I write. With no exceptions, all their teachers approve of the idea, which isn't surprising in a liberal nation like Denmark. On the appointed day, we attend a magnificent ceremony during which Djibril, my younger boy, reads a passage from the Quran. Later on I ask my older boy, Salaheddin, what he thinks of the experience. 'It's different from Baba's mosque,' he answers.

'What do you mean, "different"?'

'In the big mosque, the imams are seventy-year-old men sitting on thrones from which they never get off.'

I love this spontaneous and funny response. It pinpoints the purpose of Islamic feminism and our goal in establishing a women's mosque: deconstructing hierarchies and dismantling the 'thrones' on which the men, in a dominant position, have been monopolising the discourse for too long without considering the issues affecting Muslim women.

CHAPTER TWO

Between forest and minaret

In Damascus:

a gazelle sleeps

beside a woman

in a bed of dew

then the woman takes off her dress

and covers Barada with it!

Mahmoud Darwish, from *The Stranger's Bed*

Nothing predisposed me to becoming a woman imam. I never could have imagined such a destiny for myself. Yes, my father was born in Syria (known long ago as Bilad al-Sham or 'the northern country') and grew up in Damascus in a house in the historic part of the city, twenty yards from the Great Umayyad Mosque of Damascus. Yes, before sunrise, my grandfather Naïm, married to Wajiha and father of six children who worked hard to support his family, was a muezzin who would climb the thousand steps of the west minaret to call the faithful to prayer. I have often imagined the voice of this man I never knew rising up in the warm early morning and soaring over the Damascene rooftops, singing: 'prayer is better than sleep'. But to tell the truth, as a young girl, I pictured myself becoming an actress or a psychologist rather than an imam engaged in the intellectual fight for Islamic feminism, challenging patriarchal mindsets.

Damascus, the city where 'a gazelle sleeps beside a woman' (in the words of the Palestinian poet Mahmoud Darwish), was founded in the third century BC. Damascus, capital of a beautiful and martyred country, was devastated by seven years of an atrocious war that has already taken more than half a million lives at the time of writing; 2.7 million Syrian children do not go to school because they have either been destroyed or it's too dangerous. My father comes from there. His father, Naïm Khankan, has a small shop in the old souk. He sells shoes, nightshirts, undergarments and handkerchiefs. The family isn't well off. Among his siblings (three sisters and three brothers) my father is the only one who goes on to study at a university. While studying Arabic literature, he earns a living teaching at high school. Ambitious and entrepreneurial, he confirms his place as the intellectual in the family by writing for various newspapers and publishing a book of short stories, titled *Strangers When We Met*. The title is prophetic, announcing his immanent love story with my mother many years later in Denmark. Naïm dies without warning in 1967 while fasting for Ramadan. My father finds him in the early morning, sitting and crying. He looks weak. My father brings fruit to his bedside and my grandfather tells him: 'Go in peace, Allah will give you the fruit of Paradise.'

My father goes into the city to look for his brothers and sisters, and when he returns home, all the doors are open. He knows his father is dead. When a person dies, it is customary to leave all the doors of a house open in order to allow the soul to take flight. Then in 1970, my father loses his mother to a stroke. It is not long after the death of the Egyptian president Gamal Abdel Nasser, who was loved by many Syrians, including my father.

During the 1966 coup d'état which brought Hafez al-Assad to power, whose reign would last thirty years until his death in 2000 (with his son Bashar becoming his successor), my father finds himself aligned with the regime's adversaries due to his political activism and criticism of the government in a series of articles published by clandestine outlets. However, the mukhabarat, the secret police, establishes a climate of terror and the disappearances of those in the opposition multiply. My father sells all 150 copies of his book and flees to Denmark, planning to later join his close activist friends.

On a cold December night in 1970, my father reaches Copenhagen, the capital of the little kingdom of Denmark and then home to 5 million people. He has travelled by car from Damascus to Aleppo, by taxi to Istanbul, by train through Bulgaria, Yugoslavia, Italy, Austria and West Germany, then finally by ship over the Baltic Sea to Copenhagen. He had wanted to go to Stockholm from there, but he lost his train ticket. A kind woman gives my father some money so that he can stay at a student hostel. The Christmas lights illuminate the streets of the capital and my father decides to remain. He has never seen such beautiful streets with so many lights. He goes to the police to turn himself in.

My mother comes to Copenhagen on 1 January 1971 on a ship from Helsinki. She has come to visit her sister who is working in Denmark, where the economy is better than in Finland. In the second week of January, in the middle of the street, not far from the famous Tivoli Gardens amusement park, my father sees my mother, Irja, sitting and talking with her sister in a café. He approaches her and introduces himself. As they speak, she confesses that, like him, she is far away from home. At the age of twenty-one, she crossed the Baltic Sea, armed with her nurse's diploma and the hope that she could work at Frederiksberg Hospital. My parents meet two more times that same evening. First, at a restaurant where my father throws several stolen glances at my mother, and later at a dance hall. The moment she is about to leave with her sister, he finally walks towards her and asks her to dance. That very dance becomes the beginning of their future. A month later, my father asks my mother to marry him! Her answer falls hard: she refuses, of course, as she barely knows him. However, they get married after ten months, my mother having only put up a month's resistance to the charm of this generous and expressive man from the Middle East. Almost half a century later, they still form the strong and admirable couple who serve as an inspiring example for me. Every day their union reminds me how much the 'clash of civilisations' can be a fertile melding, a complementary enrichment. My mother is Christian and my father is Muslim. This rarely posed a problem for them, and when it did, my parents sought a point of convergence. Love is a process, an alloy of compromise and negotiation. I am the product of this wise philosophy. Half Finnish, half Syrian, my identity is there: an intersection. I am the East and the West. The village and the city. The refugee and the protected. I am a synthesis balanced on a tightrope. A product of Finland and Syria who came into existence in Denmark in 1974.

For a child, this in-between position isn't always comfortable. Many mixed-race or bicultural children can attest to this: their search for their identity is more difficult, alternating between doubt and melancholy. Intuitively, they search for simple schemas that can provide clear answers to their questions. When they become adults, this complexity transforms into a richness. For me, it forms the basis for my political action. It allows me to adapt to any situation. I always look at things from several angles and I can naturally bring opposites into agreement. Differences don't bother me. I know that the world is never black or white. It is grey, nuanced and at the same time … so colourful.

I've never defined myself by a national identity. Nation states are a human invention. When we're born, it's not written on our foreheads that we're Danish, Syrian, Pakistani, French or German. I am a citizen of the world. My home is where my family is, or where I feel I am part of a community, where I give and receive love. Passports or genes have little to do with it. Some Danes consider themselves to be citizens above others. They pretend to love their country more than others based on an absurd syllogism: 'I prefer my family to my friends, my friends to my neighbours, my neighbours to my compatriots, my compatriots to Europeans, Europeans to Muslims.' This 'love' of Denmark has nothing authentic about it. As Kierkegaard wrote, this love is ultimately a sophisticated form of love for oneself. Yet Denmark occupies a special place in my heart. During my prolonged stays in Syria and Egypt, I always felt homesick. Denmark is where I was born, where I grew up, where most of my family and friends live.

Denmark is also the country that welcomes my father in the early 1970s. The far right is still marginal and foreigners are seen as an asset to the economy. Not long after he arrives, my father stays with a host family. He quickly learns Danish and can becomes fluent in the language. He opens a small perfume store, then sells it in order to have a stab at an enterprise he deems more promising: the restaurant industry. And so our patronym goes up in big golden letters on a busy pedestrian street in the centre of the city. Kankan

– 'Middle Eastern cuisine', as the sign specifies – is located a few blocks away from what will become Mariam Mosque. It's an immediate success, not only because of the quality of the food (the Syrian dish *shish taouk*, chicken marinated in a type of lemon aioli then grilled, is irresistible), but also thanks to Baba's warm welcome. At the weekend, it's not unusual for me to spend a good part of the day and evening there with my sister Nathalie. We help with everything, in the kitchen and the dining room, all the while listening to the other exiles' passionate discussions about the politics of the Middle East and its leaders, like King Hussein in Jordan, Anwar el-Sadat in Egypt and Saddam Hussein in Iraq. They often speak about the fate of the Palestinians, the war in Libya and the one between Iran and Iraq. I soak it all in.

My parents buy a house in a residential neighbourhood outside Copenhagen, thirty minutes from the restaurant. What a privilege to spend one's childhood in a stable environment! At school I am an excellent student and often assert my independent, intrepid nature. My mother often says that my sister and I are like the sun and the moon: I am the sun and my sister, now holder of a PhD and lecturer in Arabic language and literature at the University of Berkeley, the moon. Different and complementary, we are as close to each other today as we were growing up. Nathalie is my inspiration, my grounding and the person with whom I laugh the most.

I have a burning passion for the theatre. At the age of seven, I begin my career as a playwright. Before an audience of three – Mama, Baba and my sister Nathalie – I write and stage a play in three acts. Its title: 'The Bank Robber Shows Up in His Underwear'. The inspiration came from Mary Poppins and Pippi Longstocking. Like many Scandinavian children, I admire Pippi, the tenacious orphan girl invented by Swedish novelist Astrid Lindgren, to whom Nordic feminism owes a great deal. In Lindgren's books, generations learned that girls can impose their rules on boys. Pippi is capable of lifting a horse with one hand, standing up to adults, living all alone in a big house aged seven, stopping robbers and whirling them around in the air before handing them over to the police. I'm very much inspired by Pippi's famous saying 'I've never tried that before, so I'm sure I can do it!'

As a teenager, my passion for the stage does not diminish. I participate in a high-school theatre troop, playing the brave Aslaug Sigurdsdatter from the Viking saga of Ragnar Lodbrog. I also take on roles in well-known Scandinavian plays by Henrik Ibsen and August Strindberg, but also venture to further horizons like *The House of Bernada Alba* by the Spaniard Federico García Lorca, in which I play the young and rebellious Adela, in love with the handsome Pepe el Romano. Dancing, reading and music, especially Michael Jackson, are my pastimes. Even today, at home or alone in my hotel room when I'm giving talks abroad about Islamic feminism and Mariam Mosque, I dance, turning my dress in one direction, then the other, like a whirling dervish. I must still be ten years old.

After school I play with the girls in class and my neighbourhood. My friends are named Sine, Anne Mette, Camilla, Maria and Pernille. In 2016, I learned through the press that Pernille founded a small political party on the Islamophobic far right. Further right than the Danish People's Party, which is already quite xenophobic, the New Right (Nye Borgerlige) is currently a hot topic of discussion in Denmark. A month after it was formed, the polls already attributed 5 per cent of voting intentions to the party. According to my childhood friend, Islam is a threat to Danish society; our country must therefore harden our immigration policies, which are already restrictive, and accelerate deportations. I feel sad when I think back on all the good moments I had with her. When we got home from primary school, we did our homework together, as close as two curious and mischievous children could be. I taught her everything I knew because she was a year below me. One day her teacher even told my mother that I had to stop teaching her, since she had become too clever for her class.

When I turned ten, her family moved away and I never saw her again. I didn't hear anything about her until the party was created. Then she mentioned our friendship in the media and on Facebook. I sent her a private message telling her that I'd love to meet with her in person, but I didn't respond to the media. In any case, the buzz started. Dozens of journalists offered to interview me about Pernille; some wanted to organise a debate between us. Just imagine: two childhood friends meeting for the first time in thirty years, one an imam and the other a far-right politician! I declined. I manage my communication down to the inch and always remain in charge of my own schedule. In the meantime, I left a message on Pernille's voicemail to tell her I wasn't opposed to meeting on neutral ground, but without journalists. She wanted to meet with me as well, and I truly think she was sincere in her wish to reunite. But politics came between us, and when I spoke out publicly against her political ideas, she didn't call me back.

One day when I'm nine years old, my father teaches me an important lesson. Seated in the big armchair in the living room, he stops reading *Berlingske Tidende*, the leading Danish newspaper, and asks me to come over to him. Out of the blue, he asks me a puzzling question, coming from someone who has rarely spoken about religious subjects with me: 'What do you believe in? What is your religion?' His expression is unusually serious. I remain silent, unable to come up with the least response. My father then grows very angry, the clamour beating down on me like thunderbolts from Valhalla, the Vikings' paradise. I don't remember his words, but my sister, aged eleven, told me later he was in an irrational state, as if our father was suddenly feeling guilty of having turned his back on his religion and neglecting to make us good Muslims. He and my mother had actually decided that we would have a double religious education, both Muslim and Christian, and would be able to choose freely when we became adults. Compared to that of Muslim children, our Islamic education looked like a spiritual no man's land. 'If you believe in nothing, you *are* nothing!' he had yelled before calming down. This episode made an indelible impression on me.

From that point, I started questioning myself. From time to time, a voice inside me would ask: 'What do you believe in?' This question pursued me for a long time. I didn't have an answer, because I'd grown up with the idea that you should be fully aware of your own mind when making choices, and that you should only become a believer by making the decision to be one. Like love, faith doesn't impose itself on anyone. Loving and believing are individual choices that demand action, progression. I truly desired religion. But I didn't make the choice until the end of adolescence.

The years pass, punctuated by summer holidays at my grandmother's farm in Finland. She lives in Mahlu, a small village in the countryside, near the city of Jyväskylä in the centre of the country. Getting there is an expedition that takes three days, driving almost 2,000 miles towards the Arctic Circle through forests of birches and firs. On the way, we stop over at the home of my mother's sister Sylvi and her family in Sweden, as Sylvi's husband is Swedish. Then the family Volvo heads back into the forest. Firs, birches, lakes: the countryside is infinite and we swim in any lakes we find along the way. At these latitudes, nature penetrates the senses, fashions mentalities and creates the conditions for a distinctive Scandinavian mysticism connected to the four elements: fire, water, air and earth. Gazing out of the window, my mind wanders, imagining the inhabitants of these forests, trolls devoting themselves to collecting wild berries and mushrooms, in the undergrowth of the abundant ferns. Up there in the north, the summer sun doesn't set, even at midnight. Finally, we head due south across the 'land of a thousand lakes' to reach my grandmother's village, 250 more miles away.

The farm is inhabited by the spirit of my grandmother, Eeva, the anchor of the family who has an iron character, yet who is nevertheless sweet, mild and welcoming. She knew war at a very young age. During the winter of 1939–1940, her marriage had to be postponed because Olavi, her future husband, left for the front where the Finnish were fighting a heroic battle (though they were vilified after the war because they were seen as having fought on the 'wrong side'). At odds of one against ten, they achieved a considerable victory against the Soviet army. After the armistice in spring 1940, the solid six-foot peasant Olavi returned to the farm. He and Eeva had eight children, including my mother. In the big white house, everyone would help with the household chores and the work on the farm. At the age of twelve, my mother knew how to cook for ten people. My mother is also a rock.

One day I asked her about how she brought up my sister and me. Her answer pleased me: 'I raised you without raising you,' she said with typical Finnish brevity. She means by this that she never gave in to the temptation to project her own ambitions, desires, beliefs or dreams on to us. In no way did she try to direct us, manipulate us or indoctrinate us. She was content to give us a framework and watch us grow. This might seem like passivity, but it's actually the opposite: a restrained discipline bordering on asceticism. My grandmother Eeva did the same with her eight children, and I try to practise the same thing with my two girls and two boys. Too often, childhood can be summarised by eighteen years of prohibitive rules and barriers that block self-affirmation, turn off the taste for initiative and prevent one's true personality from hatching. The Christian Lebanese poet and philosopher Kahlil Gibran (1883–1931) wrote a magnificent poem on the subject titled 'On Children', which appeared in his work *The Prophet*, my favourite book as a teenager. All parents should meditate on it. He says things better than anyone else:

> *And a woman who held a babe against her bosom said, 'Speak to us of Children.'*
> *And he said:*
> *Your children are not your children.*

They are the sons and daughters of Life's longing for itself.

They come through you but not from you,

And though they are with you, yet they belong not to you.

You may give them your love but not your thoughts.

For they have their own thoughts.

You may house their bodies but not their souls,

For their souls dwell in the house of tomorrow, which you cannot visit,
*   not even in your dreams.*

You may strive to be like them, but seek not to make them like you.

For life goes not backward nor tarries with yesterday.

You are the bows from which your children as living arrows are sent forth.

The archer sees the mark upon the path of the infinite, and He bends you
*   with His might that His arrows may go swift and far.*

Let your bending in the Archer's hand be for gladness;

For even as He loves the arrow that flies, so He loves also the bow that
*   is stable.*

With its crystal-clear light, its reviving air, its days that go on forever and its starry nights, nothing compares to a Scandinavian summer, especially in Finland. We spend all day playing ball, hide-and-seek and tag. In the company of my sister, my two favourite cousins from Denmark and our numerous Finnish cousins, we go off on adventures in the forest, picking bilberries and strawberries, watching the ants and earthworms climbing through the moss under the ferns. We go swimming, practically naked, in the surrounding lakes, then dry off in the sun. We put our clothes back on, lying in the tall grass, watching the clouds moving in big convoys across the blue sky towards the east, in the direction of St Petersburg. We go line fishing. And, back at Grandpa Olavi and Grandma Eeva's house, we climb up the haystacks before hurtling down them, in forward rolls and a concert of laughter. Moments of grace! Before we go to bed, we visit the sauna, located in an old house across from my grandparents' house. We run from house to house in our bare feet.

The summer I am ten, in 1984, marks our first holiday in Syria. By greasing the palm of a well-placed civil servant at the Ministry of Interior, my father erases all traces of his past political activities: he is no longer on the blacklist of those who oppose the regime. He can go back to his country without the fear of being troubled by the mukhabarat. I finally discover the Syria he has told us so much about, in Damascus, the city of white stone, with its dry climate, set on a plateau fifty miles from the sea. My sister and I are well behaved and dressed nicely in skirts with European hats. At the airport, we meet our Syrian family – and I immediately receive ten thousand wet kisses. These people are strangers, and yet they feel so close. I try to dry my face from the kisses and my eyes from the tears. We arrive at the home of one of my father's cousins with a trunk full of presents: hats, dresses and gold jewellery. The first day is devoted to distributing the presents to my father's uncles, aunts and cousins, whom I meet for the first time. My father is truly Father Christmas, emptying the contents of his sack over glasses of mint tea. An unforgettable memory.

I'm intrigued by my new large family, whose numerous members seem so close. In a single day, my family multiplies by ten. I'm fascinated by the feeling of belonging to such a large group in which I feel so much love and solidarity. This is where my desire to have a big family one day is born, a dream that has since come to pass. My father sees things differently. On returning to Copenhagen, he describes the opposite situation to us. According to him, large families can be crushing, and living in western Europe is a chance to protect us from having our private life continually interrupted. After over a decade in Denmark, there's no doubt he has adapted to Western culture.

Another thing strikes me in Damascus: the omnipresence of armed men. I see police officers and soldiers with machine guns. For a child who grew up in Scandinavian society, so stable and peaceful, this sight is strange. I remember the giant portraits of President Hafez al-Assad all over the city and its stores. My father brought his new video camera with him to Damascus. He loves filming. Even today, he has the complete collection of my theatre performances, immortalised on VHS cassettes, carefully lined up on a shelf in his office. In Damascus he films everything that appears before his eyes: buildings, people, his cousins. On the third day, he takes a long travelling shot, capturing on film the streets of the capital along the road that takes us, by car, to the home of another cousin in the suburb of Beit Arab.

Suddenly someone knocks on the door. The agents of the mukhabarat, the secret police, burst into the room and drag away my parents, as well as one cousin, in an uproar of shouts, cries and Quran recitations. My sister and I stay there, overwhelmed with anxiety, feeling all the more lost as we cannot speak Arabic. Communication is established in rudimentary English with the few members of our family who can speak a little of the language. In the afternoon, our parents and my father's cousin are released. Apart from the cousin having been beaten, everything returns to normal after the regime's agents have watched the entirety of my father's video recordings to confirm that he was not a spy, but a citizen turned tourist filming Damascus for his own enjoyment.

Despite this traumatic event, the rest of the holiday enchants me. I am amazed by the beauty of the old Damascene houses and the mosques, intoxicated by the smell of spices in the alleys of the souk, won over by the Mediterranean climate. In the Middle East, I feel at home, in harmony with myself. With my cousins, I communicate through gestures, laughter, facial expressions. I've always known the art of contact. Everywhere, my mother is welcomed with overwhelming kindness. A few aunts and uncles insist she convert to Islam, but always with tact. Syria claims to be a parliamentary democracy, but it is actually a dictatorship, dominated since 1963 by the Ba'ath

Party (Arab Socialist Ba'ath Party – Syria Region). It recognises the leading role of Islam in the rise of the Arab nation, but believes that only a secular state will allow all the members of an Arab nation, deeply divided in terms of beliefs, to unite.

In any case, discovering Syria makes a deep impression on me. When we return to Copenhagen, I affirm my identity, quite differently from that of my classmates, with the sense that my singularity constitutes a great source of cultural wealth. During my adolescence, we return to Syria several times, which allows my double identity to blossom a little more with each visit. However, my adolescence itself is identical to that of other Danish teens. I often go swimming in the sea, I shut myself up in my bedroom with my girlfriends to talk for hours, I walk through the streets of Copenhagen. We go to the movies to see *The Last Emperor* and *Rain Man*, or classics like *A Streetcar Named Desire*, the adaptation of the play by Tennessee Williams starring Marlon Brando. I love melodramas: they bring out my romantic side. Action films have never interested me.

When I turn fifteen, I start working at Kankan on Fridays and Saturdays, helping out in the dining room and kitchen. I discover professional life, watching the chef work while I earn a little money. After hours the whole staff dines as a family. My father's table is always open, and almost always joined by friends from various horizons and countries. The animated and often political conversations are enriching. As an adult, I have kept this lifestyle: at my house, I keep a generous table and neighbours and friends show up as they please, forming big groups of people and creating animated meals.

Despite my having come of age, my religious inclination still hasn't transformed into faith. I rarely go to mosque; on the other hand, I start attending concerts in churches. While listening to Handel's Mass in B Minor or programmes of sacred music by Bach under the vaulted ceilings of some religious building, a little voice speaks to me: 'What do you believe in?' Faith is not something that strikes like lightning. It's a slow-acting elixir that depends on multiple factors: cultural milieu, education, meetings, chance, destiny, coincidences. It also depends on the plan God has formulated for you.

At nineteen, my horizon opens up. I start to believe. This is the time in my life when I meet some young practising Muslims, including a spiritual kung fu teacher who prays five times a day and, of course, doesn't drink alcohol. His individuality, devotion and discipline inspire me. I take kung fu classes with him in the lively neighbourhood (now trendy and hipster) of Nørrebro. He explains that he is on the Sufi path, the way of inner wisdom that, at the heart of Islam, embodies openness, respect and a sense of brother- and sisterhood that goes beyond class, gender, race and religion. My meeting with this kung fu and Sufi teacher is the first step on my journey towards experiencing Islam. I'm an idealist in search of the absolute. I've always loved taking things seriously, and never given any thought to the possibility of being in a relationship without imagining marriage as the end result. In the same way, I love the principle according to which one must abstain from having sexual relations outside the sacred bond of marriage. This isn't prudishness, but rather a way of protecting one's heart and sheltering it from being hurt. We must take care of our souls, just like we take care of our bodies.

After high school, when the time comes to choose what I will study in college, I hesitate between acting, psychology and religion. In the end, I choose the history of religions option at the University of Copenhagen, with the sociology of religions and contemporary Islam as my focus. It's an instinctive choice. I feel that I must answer my spiritual questions. In the same vein, I begin studying the Arabic language, which soon leads me to Egypt, during a six-month stay in Cairo and, once more, Syria.

At the age of nineteen, I am ready to abandon my Christian name and only use my Muslim nickname, officially given to me by a spiritual Muslim soulmate – my kung fu teacher on the Sufi path. I keep my last name Khankan. It is a symbolic decision. From now on, my name is no longer Ann Christine Khankan, but شيرين, or Sherin Khankan. My parents have no objections. And, from Ann Christine to Sherin, the change in sound is subtle.

CHAPTER THREE

On the road to Damascus

Love is the origin of the world and its ruler, but all its ways are filled with flowers and blood, flowers and blood.

Knut Hamsum

At the end of the 1990s, relations between the West and the Muslim world are unstable. The American war is raging against Iraq. The conflict has been prolonged by the embargo imposed by the Clinton administration on the country of Saddam Hussein, which has resulted in thousands of children dying of malnutrition in hospitals in the Middle East. Algeria is beset by civil war, and the attacks in France perpetrated by the Armed Islamic Group (GIA) sow fear. In the Balkans, the war in former Yugoslavia pits the minority Serbs against the Kosovar Albanians, who are Muslims.

While these events appear far from those of my generation, they strongly affect my fellow students in the sociology of religions at the University of Copenhagen, as they do me. The tremors of the 'new world order' arising with the end of the Cold War excite our interest, and I become immersed in their details in order to try to understand them. I'm so happy with what I've chosen to study – each hour in class confirms the logic of my choice! However, my father is worried about the subjects my sister Nathalie and I have chosen. She is one of twelve students to study Arabic at the University of Copenhagen. 'Religion and Arabic,' he says. 'What will become of you both? What will you do in the future?' He would have preferred for us to study law or another subject that would lead to a more stable career. 'A woman has to be independent and provide for herself,' he often says.

After deciding to write my thesis on Sufism and Islamic activism, I add Standard Arabic to my studies at Copenhagen University. I then leave for Egypt together with Rasmus Alenius Boserup, a friend from my Arabic class (who later becomes the director of the Danish Egyptian Dialogue Institute in Cairo), to improve my speaking abilities. We both take classes at the British Council of Cairo, where I learn Standard Arabic, and work at St Andrew's Refugee Services, a Christian organisation founded in 1979 that helps African refugees and migrants who have settled in the Egyptian capital. At the age of twenty-one, I teach English to Somalian and Sudanese men and women, whose homelands are sinking into extreme political turmoil. As I walk home from work, people on the streets often point at me and call me 'Rose', in reference to the character played by Kate Winslet in the film *Titanic*, which has just come out in the Cairo cinemas (in a censored version that leaves out all the romantic scenes).

Cairo is magnetic, prodigious, overpopulated and excessive. During my first few days there on my own, I feel a little uncertain and scared. With its thousand minarets and monstrous traffic jams, the Egyptian capital balances between history and modernity. I check in at an old historic hotel in central Cairo and prepare myself for this new life in a strange city with an unfamiliar language. The next day, I rent an apartment on the left bank of the Nile in Giza, not far from the pyramids, in the Mohandessin district, where many of the foreign embassies are located. The landlady, Dr Sohair, is a charismatic Coptic Christian, who says she's overjoyed to meet me. 'I really don't want to rent to Muslims,' she specifies, describing her previous tenants, some 'very impolite' Saudis. I then explain to her that, actually, I am Muslim. She reconsiders, decides to grant me the lease, and we end up becoming very close friends.

Djihan, an Anglo-Egyptian friend with whom I study Arabic, invites me to her Egyptian family's house for the weekend, a huge farm on the edge of the Nile. We head out on horseback through the semiarid landscape, and I feel like an adventurer. In the capital, I visit the Egyptian Museum and its collection of treasures from antiquity, as well as the necropolis of Giza and its twin pyramids, Khufu and Khafre. I sometimes go to the mosques to pray. However, my faith is still only a small flame, lit but uncertain and trembling.

On returning to Copenhagen, I feel even more linked to the Arab world and I long to return and further improve my Arabic. The Danish Institute of Damascus offers me a study grant and I return to Syria, the land of my ancestors, to study Arabic at Damascus University for four months. This time I'm in Syria without my parents, and so I discover Damascus with adult eyes – its old stones, its smells, its authentic, peaceful charm, Mount Qasioun overlooking the city. Once more I am drawn to the textures and sounds and smells of Damascus, though I'm also beginning to experience what it means to live under a dictatorial regime. In 2000 – we did not know it then – Hafez al-Assad dies and his thirty-year rule ends abruptly. I visit the French Institute in Damascus, where I meet a researcher and doctoral student named Ryad Atlagh (today a professor at the Sorbonne) who becomes a very close friend. He offers me a study space next to him in his office at the Institute. He is the one who introduces me to Ibn Arabi, the great master of Sufism, who later becomes my source of inspiration and knowledge.

As agreed with my father, I stay with my cousin Muhyeddin, a judge in an administrative court. He, his wife Wafa and their three children, Dana, Hamadi and Lulu, live in the northeastern part of the city, in the district of Rukneddine. Not long after I arrive, I go out to explore the surroundings. In Damascus a woman can walk by herself without difficulties, and so I lose myself in the animated streets of the quarter, where I discover the famous Abu Nour Mosque, which will end up becoming the subject of my thesis. It is situated in the Kurdish quarter and houses a gigantic prayer room and a centre of Islamic studies with classrooms, a library, offices, apartments and a cafeteria. Since 1987 it has accommodated an institute for the instruction of the Arabic language. Initially planned for male students, it opened its doors to women as well, and this pedagogical centre quickly started welcoming students from around the world.

With its two 200-feet-tall minarets and its modern seven-storey concrete façade, the building commands respect. As I continue my wanderings, I discover another mosque. This one houses the tomb of Ibn Arabi, the father of Sufism, which will soon also play an important role in my spiritual life. An Andalusian of Arab origin, he was born in 1165 in Murcia (now Spain) and died in 1240 in Damascus. This poet, theologian and spiritual master is identified with Sufism, the spiritual path within Islam. He is known for his prolific work, having written hundreds of books, including *The Bezels of Wisdom* and *The Meccan Revelations*. Ibn Arabi is called the great master of Sufism because his spiritual writings helped to form Islamic spirituality, especially concerning *Tasawwuf* (the Sufi principles), since the thirteenth century. He is known as 'Shaykh al-Akbar' ('the greatest master' in Arabic), 'the great mystic' and 'the renewer of religion'. Ibn Arabi represents a more theoretical development of Sufism and is known for 'the methodology of the heart' and a more embracive understanding of Islam.

During the day, I work on my thesis at the French Institute for Arabic Studies in Damascus (IFEAD) and study Arabic at the University of Damascus, also located in the capital. And in the evening, we dine as a family. 'You need to eat more. You're so thin, so skinny, you don't look healthy ... ' I repeatedly get told by Wafa, who cooks up traditional dishes I find delectable. I share a room with Lulu and Hamadi, who often sleep nestled in my arms. The oldest, Dana, is studying law and practises Islam diligently, praying five times a day. (Today she is married with one son and lives in Stockholm, where the family came as refugees. Wafa, Lulu and Hamadi are still in Cairo, and the rest of the family has remained in Syria.)

Dana's faith fascinates me during my time in Cairo, and my own faith intensifies as a result. I imitate her, conforming to the prerequisites required by Islam: cleanliness of body, clothing and place; orienting my body towards the Kaaba (the most sacred place in Mecca); sincerity and authentic intention during prayer, respecting the order of the movements; solemnity and contemplation. The five prayers, each designated by a different name, happen at dawn, noon, vespers (mid-afternoon), sunset and nightfall. The dawn prayer is called *fajr*, the noon prayer *dhuhr*, the afternoon prayer *'asr*. At sunset one speaks of *maghrib* and at nightfall, *isha*.

Far from finding this constraining, I discover on the contrary a richness in such an act of voluntary submission. I love the ritual ablution preceding prayer. It's about symbolically purifying one's body, hands and feet, and from the first contact with the water, I feel like I'm opening a set of parentheses and leaving the earthly world. I try to forget my ego, my little projects and personal worries. Five times a day, I stop for a moment, go beyond myself, raise myself up towards something greater, awaken my consciousness. If, on a given day, something is bothering or tormenting me, then my soul calms and clears.

The Muslim prayers accompany a physical practice that solicits the body. In this sense, Islamic prayer is closer to Buddhism, in which meditation sessions start with adopting a particular posture. This corporeal dimension is nothing trivial; it facilitates the connection with the sacred. When I kneel and my head touches the ground, the blood circulates through my veins, I am conscious of life and I feel as close as possible to God. My body and my spirit are set free. The bad waves and negative vibrations evaporate. Fatigue and stress disappear. I forget about everything. There is no longer anything but Allah. Five times a day, I leave the earthly world and regenerate myself.

My favourite call to prayer is the *fajr* (at dawn), the suspended moment when, for a few more seconds, the city is still asleep. The call of the muezzins pulls sleepers from their dreams. Their chants rise to the starry sky like a heady polyphony that envelops the entire city. Slightly out of sync, these chants invoking the same God join together and unite in a single sonorous movement that ends up composing a nocturnal symphony, filling the infinite space under the heavenly vault. It's magnificent. I love that the call to prayer emanates from a human voice, directly touching the heart, and not the mechanism of a clock. When the call rings out, I feel as though struck by grace, and I understand why I am a Muslim.

The call, just like the prayer itself, expresses a dialectic between multiplicity and unity. The muezzins are numerous, but each one invokes the same unique God. In the same way, all believers are different but they all respond to the same call. This movement between unity (*tawhid*) and multiplicity is also felt in the movement from the kneeling position to standing. In prostrating themselves, the faithful physically feel that everything falls on the community of believers (multiplicity) but proceeds from a single God (unity) whom they address. There are many more examples: when I kneel and place my forehead on the ground (*sujud*) I feel the oneness of God, *tawhid*. But when I stand as believers do at the end of the prayer, then ritually turn my head to the right and then to the left towards my brothers and sisters, and we touch each other on the shoulders, I feel the multiplicity of God through humanity is truly being manifested. Prayer reminds me every

46

day and every moment that we cannot grasp the unity of Allah without understanding the multiplicity of what Allah created. Jews, Christians, Muslims: we all share the essential idea that God is both everywhere, hence multiple, and unique. Allah has created a world of multiplicity because He *wants* us to want multiplicity, in order that we can understand the idea of His unity. In other words, you cannot claim to love God if you do not respect your fellow human beings, regardless of faith.

Every day I return to Abu Nour Mosque before or after my Arabic classes, attracted to this 'hive' where so many women are active. Their dynamism and Islamic activism intrigue and fascinate me because, in my Syrian family, very few of the women are Muslim activists. In this sacred place, the women are in charge of the administration and logistics, direct visitors, teach Arabic classes, perform *dhikr* (Islamic meditation) and run the library, all with welcoming and joyful spirits. What if I devoted my thesis to Abu Nour Mosque? This theme has almost never been studied (other than by a German researcher named Annabelle Böttcher who worked on the subject several years earlier). It's also a unique chance to get to know the prestigious Sheikh Ahmed Kuftaro, who is well known in Syria as a Sufi figure and spiritual leader, as well as internationally for his work bringing reconciliation between Christians and Muslims. He has been directing the mosque since the 1960s. A Grand Mufti of Syria, this man, born in

1915, holds the highest position in Sunni Islam in the country. Since his death in 2004, the aura of this man, who used to evoke the convergences between Islam and Christianity, continues to radiate. But he was also accused of being a puppet for the Syrian government.

Recommended to me by one of my uncle's friends, the Grand Mufti receives me with simplicity along with a female teacher named Mukarram in the mosque. As I sit beside his bed with Mukarram, he reacts positively to my idea of moving to Syria for eight months to study his mosque and Sufi thought. When I ask him for authorisation to speak and spend time with people who work at Abu Nour Mosque, he agrees.

After four months in Damascus, I return to Copenhagen, determined to get back to Syria as quickly as possible. Always ready to support me, my parents are delighted. Six months later, my sister and I move into an apartment my father has just bought in Damascus. There is a slight problem: women are not usually allowed to live alone, without a male presence. We are able to do so thanks to my father, who wants us to have a family home and blesses our independence openly before the extended family. I feel strong and equipped, mature enough for the adult world.

Damascus enchants me. The heart of this city keeps beating long after nightfall. What a contrast with Copenhagen, where everything seems dead, turned off, after 9 p.m.! Our neighbour across the landing is named Myada. She is sweet and takes care of us. One day she catches me in the elevator wearing the *galabiyya* and the hijab. Crossing paths with me, she calls out: 'Hamdulillah mabrouk (Thanks be to God, congratulations), you're wearing the headscarf, you're a true Muslim now!' I want to answer: 'That's not what makes me a real Muslim, it's what's in my heart and my actions.' But I restrain myself so that I don't hurt this charming woman who, over time, becomes a replacement mother for me during my eight-month stay in Syria.

At the beginning of my stay, I dressed like any other Muslim woman, but without the headscarf. However, as I start my fieldwork in the mosque, I dress like the other women in order to be a natural part of the Abu Nour Mosque community. And it feels natural to me. In fact, I wear a hijab and *galabiyya* during the day, which I spend almost entirely at Abu Nour Mosque. But little by little, I start reflecting on whether I should start wearing the headscarf regularly, especially on returning to Copenhagen after my stay in Syria. In the end, I decide not to. I come to the conclusion that it is possible to be a practising Muslim without wearing the headscarf. Muslim women have different interpretations of modesty. To me, the hijab is a symbol of sincerity towards God and one's relationships to others.

Today, in Copenhagen, I only wear a hijab at the mosque, when I lead prayer or give the *khutbah* (sermon). I don't need to justify myself because no one asks me about it. Mariam Mosque is a place of pluralism. Diversity is one of our objectives. Our believers, often educated people, don't seem preoccupied with knowing whether or not I wear the hijab. It's vital that we respect each person's choices. At Mariam Mosque, three of the female imams or khatibahs wear the headscarf every day; the other two only wear it when they are at the mosque, during prayer. In this sense, we reflect reality, in that Muslim women have different interpretations of modesty, with some adopting the hijab and some who choose to do without it. This choice does not presume anything about the authenticity of their beliefs. The question of Mariam Mosque's approach to Islam surpasses any debate concerning the hijab.

At Abu Nour Mosque, I am continually fascinated by the women's activity and remain intrigued by Sheikh Ahmed Kuftaro, the Grand Mufti, who continues to advocate tolerance, open-mindedness and indulging in an ecumenical spirit. During his sermons on Fridays, he emphasises the points of similarity between the 'religions of the Book', inspired by the monotheism of the Old Testament: Judaism, Christianity and Islam. It is in Syria, and not Denmark or anywhere in the West, that I hear convincing reasoning concerning the similarities between these three religions for the first time. He speaks fine words about tolerance, typical of Sufi philosophy, which are a source of permanent inspiration for me.

It is also at Abu Nour Mosque, during a sermon delivered during the large prayer service on Fridays, that the idea of an Islamic feminism comes to my mind. Listening to the Grand Mufti's *khutbah*, I say to myself: 'Could a woman lead the Friday prayer service and, instead of a man, could a person of the opposite sex be speaking at this moment? What would happen? And why not?' In a very open manner, I ask some of the women in the mosque about it. They all respond in the same way: 'But we would have to be at the same level as the Grand Mufti.' In other words, it's impossible.

The women have internalised the idea that men should dominate women. This idea disturbs me. But it was in Syria, after all, where the idea for Mariam Mosque was born, or at least that of my fight for feminism within Islam ... even if at that point I was incapable of imagining that, one day, I myself would become an imam in northern Europe. It's not living alongside Scandinavian feminism, but rather coming in contact with the women of Abu Nour Mosque, as much as for their piety and activism as their self-censorship, that serves as my first source of inspiration. It is here, seeing these admirable, intelligent, beautiful Syrian women, that I have come to understand the importance of living out one's faith with concrete actions and daily commitments – a type of political activism.

I often think back on these women. With the war raging, they weigh heavy on my memory. Sometimes I'm asked if the seven years of atrocities and the half a million deaths have eroded my belief in God or the revolution. ... It's undeniably difficult to watch such suffering and see the world's passivity and the way people are closing their eyes to it. When the war in Syria began, my father commanded me to stay silent. Like many other Syrians in Denmark, he was terrified that my protesting against the brutal Assad regime would have consequences for our family in Damascus. It's a well-known fact that the Assad regime has spies in Denmark, who report back on any oppositionist voices. This is how a dictatorship controls its people: by spreading fear. Many years after my father fled Hafez al-Assad's regime, he is still traumatised and has transferred the same fear to me by his example.

However, I decided I couldn't stay silent after realising that, whether I spoke out or not, people were getting killed. What triggered me to break my silence was the passivity of both the West and the Arab-Muslim world, as well as the rising death toll. In January 2013, I decided to found the Syrian Opposition in Denmark (SOD) together with a group of young Syrian activists in Copenhagen, including a Danish theology student named Nikolai Vartenberg and a Syrian activist named Joseph Hamoud. The SOD is a resistance movement against the Syrian regime and supports only the part of the Syrian opposition fighting for freedom, democracy and political pluralism. Together we organise street demonstrations and conferences, actively participate in debates, write articles and challenge the leading Assad supporters in Denmark. We also organised a benefit concert in Copenhagen featuring fourteen leading Danish and international artists, including Outlandish, Lars H.U.G. and Fatma Zidan, which was attended by over 500 people. But in organising concerts and collecting clothing and money, I realied that humanitarian action isn't enough; it ends up throwing money into a bottomless pit. I believe that political action can make a real difference.

Various NGOs are involved in humanitarian work in Syria. But Denmark lacks a united political Danish-Syrian resistance movement that not only dares but is willing to take a stand on the ongoing political situation in Syria. Humanitarian aid demands both political and moral responsibility. The SOD is but a few Danish-Syrians who publicly declare their resistance to the Assad regime through different media outlets.

First of all, I define the revolution in Syria as a revolt against the Assad regime and not as a civil war. Even though 'the opposition' cannot be defined as a single group due to varying political and social ideologies, it is still possible to identify a common fight for freedom, dignity and justice within the various opposition groups, along with a common desire to fight the Assad regime. I do not define the revolution in sectarian or religious terms. All over the world, the Syrian opposition has many faces. It includes secularists, Muslims, Christians, Alawites, atheists, Kurds, secular Muslims and others. The Syrian people have long lived in peace and therefore do not take part in sectarianism.

Furthermore, I support Syrian opposition groups that aim for a Syria which treats its people indiscriminately and guarantees the safety of their rights regardless of their religion, ethnic background or political convictions. As the saying goes... Gandhi said, 'A true democracy is judged by how it treats its minorities.' After the fall of the Assad regime, the Syrian people must determine their new form of government in complete sovereignty. One of many challenges Syrians will have to face is how to establish political cooperation between the secular and religious political parties. The vital question after the revolution is not *who* should govern, but *how*. It's not about which party or which president, but rather establishing clear rules for the political game which allow for the most liberty and set the tone for democracy. When the fight is finally over, the people of Syria won't accept another tyrannical ruler from a radical, anti-democratic group, be it religious or secular.

In a society in which differing perceptions and values exist side by side, those who do not accept diversity and multiplicity as an asset to society cannot play a part in bridge building and reconciliation. The young Palestinian poet Samar Abdel Jaber wrote the following in a famous Danish literary anthology bringing together a new generation of Arab voices:

Souls cannot be imprisoned
Dreams cannot be shot down with tanks
The City will not have one colour as they wish
The City is coloured with colours like the butterflies

(From the poem 'Damascus' in
A New Day's Clarity: Young Arab Voices)

It seems vital to put pressure on all levels of the tyrannical regime of Bashar al-Assad, but the regime has proven very resistant. In fact, it's always been that way. From the beginning, the whole world should have shown its solidarity with the democratic opposition. But it didn't. Some of the tragedy stems from there. Indeed, Bashar al-Assad could have become a new democratic leader in the Middle East and been an example to other countries. Most of the Syrian people went out demonstrating on the streets, not to abandon him as president, but to revolt against tyranny, corruption and lack of democracy. But he chose to slaughter his own population.

I have often felt isolated and ashamed because, in Denmark, I find myself far from the war, incapable of doing anything useful besides offering humanitarian aid and a little political action. Clearly, it is insufficient. I feel a strong sense of solidarity with my father's country, but I am here, in Copenhagen, safe and warm with my family, my children. Be that as it may, my faith remains intact. If the sorrow and pain do not completely destroy us, they can keep us alert. In fact, I believe that they are instruments of God, destined to keep us vigilant.

In 2015, when I find myself in Istanbul for a conference on women's rights, a photography exhibition dedicated to women in the war is displayed outside where the discussions are taking place. It is a series of large-format portraits, accompanied by quotations from Syrian women describing their daily life, their suffering, the loss of their loved ones. One of the portraits grabs me: a woman my age, a mother of four, like me. I will never forget her face, or her gaze, or her words: 'There was a time when I was living in Syria', one reads. 'I was a teacher and my four children were all in school. They were healthy and happy. I was in love. My husband was at my side. We had a good life. I had everything: a country, children, a husband, work, a future, dreams. And now, everything has been taken away. When I had my children with me, a family and everything else, I never asked Allah: "Why me?" Even now that everything has disappeared and I no longer have anything, I still do not ask Allah, "Why me?"'

CHAPTER FOUR

Being a Muslim woman in Europe

British Journalist: 'Mr. Gandhi, what do you think of Western civilisation?'

Gandhi: 'I think it would be a good idea'.

When I return to Europe after a year in Damascus, I'm not quite the same. Like me, the century has changed; in the summer of 2001, the political stage is peaceful. Walking through the streets of Copenhagen, my mind is elsewhere, steeped in the sounds and scents of the East – my soul stayed there. I miss the mountains, the warm late nights out in a city that rarely sleeps, the call to prayer in the early morning and the mosques on every corner, the Arab voices and singing, my family, sleeping next to little Lulu and Hamadi, new friends and the feeling of belonging to a community as I had in Abu Nour Mosque and with my Syrian family and new friends. I feel lost, alone in my own country, without a community or a home. I can't seem to find the human warmth I now desperately need. Everything here seems lacking in flavour and intensity. The superficiality annoys me. I feel a profound sense of emptiness. I'd love to test the boundaries of this place and find a community of people who would open their arms and their hearts to me, like at Abu Nour Mosque. But wherever I look, I can only see individualism and isolation. In a community, magical things can happen. My stay in Syria strengthened this belief.

In August 2001, after a few months in Copenhagen and with my thesis on Sufism and Islamic activism written, I decide to take inspiration from the women of action I met in Damascus. So I get to work creating the Forum for Critical Muslims, an association that will give Danish Muslims a pluralistic voice both inside and outside Muslim communities. The Forum is established by a small group of Muslims, including a medical doctor, Khurram Jamil, and a lecturer at Aalborg University, Henrik Plaschke. We are one month away from 9/11, which proves that this Forum is not a reaction to the terrorist attacks in New York, but rather a positive initiative, showing an awareness of the necessity of both establishing a place of worship with female Muslim leadership for practising Muslims in Denmark and a platform for debate within the Danish Muslim intellectual community, whose voice is hardly heard. I want to start a dialogue between Muslims and the rest of society. The Forum for Critical Muslims is exactly that: a voice and a face. Or rather, voices and faces.

In bringing together practising Danish Muslims, a large number of whom, like me, have an academic background, I hope to create an intellectual circle capable of elevating the debate on Islam in Denmark. It's an unprecedented initiative, since Muslims live in many different realities and the various Muslim associations are separate from each other. We bring together minds from different horizons: Sunni Muslims, Shi'ites, Alawites, Sufis and even the Ahmadi minority. Ahmadiyya is an Islamic reform movement founded by Mirza Ghulum Ahmad at the end of the nineteenth century in Punjab, India, when it was still under British rule. Persecuted in several Muslim countries, the Ahmadis, who number several million around the world, were declared to be non-Muslim by the Organisation of the Islamic Conference in 1973. And the constitution of Pakistan has denied that they are Muslims since 1974. As for us, we count three Ahmadis among the 150 'critical Muslims' in our fledgling association, which has kindled hope and pride from the beginning.

Moved by a strong sense of open-mindedness and convinced that unity brings strength, we come together to debate current events and the situation of Danish Muslims. Sometimes we meet in the historic building of the Vartov conference centre in the heart of Copenhagen, and we host monthly meetings in private homes that introduce a rereading of the Islamic texts through a spiritual approach to the Quran, which is led by visiting guest teachers, including Amér Majid, the author behind the new Danish translation of the Quran. The Forum for Critical Muslims attracts a new generation of Muslim academics, due to our theological discussions on topics such as 'Islam and Secularism', 'Reformist Islam' and 'Sufism and Islamic Feminism'. The Forum is mainly composed of college students in their twenties and early thirties.

At the time, an anti-Muslim atmosphere is rising up from the depths of society, supported in Denmark by the rise of the far-right political party Dansk Folkeparti (Danish People's Party). It is urgent to bring the Danish Muslim elite out of its ghetto so that they can speak to and speak for themselves. The 'critical Muslims' will exist in the public sphere and, I'm already convinced, will demonstrate that our community can coexist with the society to which they already belong, whatever the far right may say!

I should specify that the term 'critical' has nothing negative about it. It is used in the sense of 'constructive critique' and 'self-critique', which forms a prerequisite to any desire for improvement and development. In fact, in the Arabic language, the word *naqd* or 'critique' is a positive term that falls within the Islamic tradition of the dynamic quest for betterment. I take inspiration from the Iranian philosopher and theologian Abdolkarim Soroush. A well-known thinker and professor who was invited to speak at George Washington University in Washington, D.C., Soroush played a very active role in the Iranian revolution against the Shah's dictatorship before turning against it when he saw its fatal consequences. His thought essentially turns around the distinction between religion and religiosity. If the Quran, as the infallible and universal word of God, is religion, we must be wary of religiosity and the interpretation of the Quran by humankind, who are by essence imperfect and fallible.

The Forum is a reformist activist movement of Sufi inspiration and orientation that calls for a pluralist and democratic Islam through a spiritual rereading of the Quran and a recognition of the diversity of religious sensibilities. In our eyes, religion must not impose itself on political decisions, only inspire them. Reciprocally, politics must not dictate its requirements to religions. In every case, politics and religion must be separate. But at the same time, religion can inspire societies. After all, both politics and religion are based on what people value. We are therefore in favour of the equality of men and women, an Islamic principle put forward in the 'Farewell Sermon' by the Prophet Muhammad in 632, and later developed in Scandinavia, where women received the right to vote in 1906 in Finland, in 1913 in Norway, in 1915 in Denmark and in 1921 in Sweden. Even better, for the first time, we are advancing the idea that women can become imams – which prefigures Femimam, the association I will create fifteen years later, which will give birth to Mariam Mosque. In the meantime, the Forum is already the first and only Danish Muslim association with a woman spokesperson.

In brief, the 'critical Muslims' represent an original, creative force with a nuanced voice and perspectives that are balanced and progressive.

In practice, the project is both simple *and* ambitious: organising meetings, debates, seminars and conferences on the Quran and Islam, as well as offering counselling for women through Islamic spiritual care. We want to show that our religion is not a threat but, far from it, represents a fact that must be counted on both now and in the future. With the other members of the Forum, the majority of whom come from the universities of Copenhagen, we agree to produce quality intellectual work in the form of written texts, in particular opinion articles in the 'Debates' pages in the main Danish newspapers that discuss subjects such as Islam and the situation in the Middle East.

As I have already said, the East and not the West is the source of inspiration for the Forum for Critical Muslims. In fact, the association is the product of my reflections that began in college, then developed during my stays in Arab countries. As I deepen my knowledge of Islam by refining my understanding of the Prophet Muhammad's message, I feel a growing need to define and explain my Muslim identity. I sense that non-Muslims are uncomfortable with Islam due to their poor understanding of the history of religions and their simplified idea of our religion as formed by the media – even some of the politicians on the left seem to misunderstand Islam. The most curious thing is that Western Muslims themselves seem ill at ease, to the point that some have wrongly interiorised the idea that 'living one's Muslim faith' and 'opening up to a democratic secular society' are contradictory, even incompatible, notions. As a result, some practise a rigid, conservative understanding of Islam. Can this be explained by the fact that, for too long, Muslims have been suspected, stigmatised and treated poorly in general by the media and certain right-wing politicians? By remaining silent, too many Muslim associations are conforming to such erroneous discourse, according to which democracy and Islam are not made to get along.

On the other hand, the 'critical Muslims' intend to debate the changing world and bring the question of Islam and pluralism to the Muslim community. Our goal: freeing the majority of sincere believers caught in the crossfire between the Danish People's Party, which defines Islam as a religion that is primitive and hostile to womankind and, at the other extreme, the radical Islamists, who deny parliamentary democracy and only recognise a single legislator: God. We are going to take the floor, invert this proposition and challenge these tragic messages, which in monopolising the truth, set themselves up as moral judges and act like ministers of doctrine on the back of society by appropriating the right to assign the good and bad points, and by distinguishing the 'good' Muslims from the 'bad' ones.

Contrary to this Manicheism, we want to promote plurality within Islam and maintain a special form of *adab* (meaning 'sensitivity', 'good manners' and 'affection'), respect and cohesion among our members, without discriminating against anyone, and whilst acknowledging different sensibilities and the diverse paths to God. One of God's messages, the tawhid, actually expresses the idea of diversity in unity. Far from proposing a uniform view of the world, Islam expects every Muslim to fight for diversity and to seek to understand each other by focusing their efforts on the *tawhid* and recognising the specificity of each person. In this, the Quran is a vehicle for universal values.

I like to write, and I write a lot. Running on the momentum of my thesis, I produce texts on different ideas connected to Islam. So I write a manifesto, founding act, or plan, for the Forum for Critical Muslims. In 2006, I publish 'A Muslim Manifesto' in the Danish newspaper *Politiken*, which explains the idea behind the Forum for Critical Muslims. The seed for female imams is planted in this manifesto, as for the first time I publish my vision of a mosque with female imams.

Today, almost two decades later, I am not afraid to use the terms 'imam' and 'imamah'. Then, I was. In the manifesto, I use the term 'khatibah' (the woman who delivers the sermon) instead of 'imam' in order to describe my dream of a mosque with female leadership. The manifesto is addressed to those for whom the Quran is the manifestation of the word of

God and who believe it can transform us from the moment when we seek essence beyond the text. 'This Forum', I write, 'is for all those whose actions are not motivated by the hope for Paradise or the fear of Hell, but purely out of selfless devotion to the Creator. Selfish calculations cannot serve the engine of faith.' I continue: 'Our path to faith allows for the flourishing of an enormous spiritual potential and leads to the development of our selves. Finding this path frees us as human beings. Humility, inner purity and gratitude are the pillars that support us as we walk towards our hearts. This Forum is for those who desire to awaken their consciences before dying.'

I add: 'The Forum is open to all those who believe in universal values and favour what unites human beings rather than what separates them. Everything is a matter of choice. If we choose what unites us, then we can transform the current world and make it better. Islam is a vital inspiration, not a decree.' And finally: 'This Forum is addressed to you who do not judge others, but strive to reconcile the irreconcilable; to you who consider human beings as your brothers and sisters, independent of their religion or nationality. Being at once an authentic believer and a staunch democrat is entirely possible. It is a universal concept, independent of nationalities, religions and geography.'

The Forum for Critical Muslims rests on four principles: reason, renewal, critique and multiplicity. The first signifies that, instead of blindly imitating the interpretation of the Quran proposed by certain Muslims, we must encourage individuals to use their reason to study the Quran for themselves. God gifted us with intelligence; it seems right for us to use it to bring to life the word God has revealed to us. However, this process requires us to rely on a guide who possesses knowledge. Each one of us must interpret the Quran and bring it to life by finding the right balance between reason and emotions (the heart). Some verses of the Quran are clear and explicit, others require interpretation. Just like the most illustrious Muslim scholars and legal experts, we must practice *ijtihad*, the effort personal reflection that aims to interpret the fundamental texts of Islam. By mobilising our intelligence, and not blindly repeating set phrases, we can understand the Prophet's life and draw a rational interpretation from the Quran corresponding to the moral, philosophical, political and spiritual values of our time: equality of the sexes, races, nationalities, social classes and religions. We must engage our reason in the service of *tafsir*, the exegesis of the sacred text. This means discovering, understanding, clarifying, revealing and explaining what is masked or hidden in order to live out one's faith in a dynamic adapted to today's world. *Ijtihad* and *tafsir* are essential tools for those who wish to understand the message of God, whose counsel is at once mandatory and subject to interpretation.

The Quran and the Prophet Muhammad encourage all men and women, at every moment, to make the effort to work and raise themselves up through knowledge; they do not demand the blind repetition of a dogma. One day, a man asks the Prophet who the greatest scientist is. The latter's response is categorical: 'It is the one who always tries to learn from others, like a student who is thirsty for new knowledge.' Faith without knowledge is vain (the inverse is also true). Simply reciting the Quran without researching its deep meaning is pointless.

The second pillar supports the idea of renewal, revival and rereading. This is the raison d'être of the Forum for Critical Muslims. At its heart, our actions aim to reread, contextualise and adapt the Muslim understanding of the Quran for contemporary times. In Arabic the term *al-Nahda*, among other meanings, references the rebirth, or the 'revival' of Islam. Believers who wish to progress must first recognise their ignorance and their limits in understanding the Quran. This approach supposes a certain amount of humility and the sincere intention to improve. The 'critical Muslims' start from this premise. Thanks to our activities, discussions and intellectual output, we aim at bettering ourselves. This work allows us to qualify the image of Islam by putting us in a position of humility and facilitating a dialogue between Muslims and non-Muslim Westerners.

Working for the revival of Islam means reconsidering Islamic civilisation's contribution to global culture, a contribution that has unfortunately been neglected. Too many people ignore Muslim authors, scientists, theologians and philosophers throughout history. Our ambition is to increase their visibility by emphasising their notable absence in school curricula and college syllabi. When I studied philosophy, I wasn't taught anything about their efforts, discoveries or written works. Many Europeans believe that Muslims have not contributed anything valuable to Western civilisation, other than translating the works of Aristotle. But this is not the case. For example, the oldest university in the world (continually operating to this day) is the University of Al Quaraouiyine in Fez, Morocco, founded in 859 AD. The Muslim contribution to world culture is not nil, but rather denied. Islam is at the heart of philosophy, science and Sufi thought. So many of the great ideas that have been ignored are worth sharing, and would contribute in bringing together the East and the West.

History is always written by 'the victors', who produce a 'dominant discourse' which, by virtue of its nature, lacks objectivity. Yet there is a certain hypocrisy in the writing of history. Some episodes are pushed to the fore and glorified, while other, more disturbing, chapters are hidden. For example, the German monk and theologian Martin Luther (1483–1546) is often presented as a great reformer, with little mention of his hatred for Jews and Muslim Turks. Who would dare to say – and who even knows – that he is the author of one of the most anti-Semitic texts in history, 'Von den Juden und ihren Lügen' ('On the Jews and Their Lies'), which laid the ideological foundations for anti-Semitism and the

Nazis 450 years later? Martin Luther is an inspiration when it comes to challenging the priesthood, and he shows that it is possible for a single person to change existing patriarchal structures. He also inspires me when it comes to going back to the religious sources and creating change from there. But we must not forget the dark chapters of his life in order to avoid categorising Jews or Muslims as secondhand people.

Revival is also, of course, for women. The Forum wants to give them more visibility, considering how underrepresented they are in the leadership of religious institutions and in the public debate. People who possess knowledge, no matter their gender, must be allowed to share it with an audience, masculine or feminine. The determining factor is their knowledge, not their gender. One of the Forum's ideas – at the time evoked as a far-off goal – consists of opening mosques where the officiating *khatibah* (the Arabic term for those who deliver the sermon) can be female. Besides the Friday prayers, these women would deliver the *khutbah* (sermon) to a female assembly. In our minds, the presence of female speakers reinforces the harmony and equality of the sexes. This would send a strong message of solidarity, fraternity and cooperation to the following generations, no matter their gender. There is nothing unusual about this revolutionary project: at Mecca, the absolute symbol of faith, devotion and abolition of social boundaries, do men and women not walk around the Kaaba together?

From the moment the organisation is launched, some Muslims question me. Why 'critical'? Why 'critical Muslims'? Are we a group of protesting activists? I reassure them. Mutually critiquing each other and accepting the opposing argument are essential steps for anyone who wants to move forward in understanding and lifting themselves up intellectually and spiritually. This ambition forces you to reformulate your point of view, to reflect on it further. Danish Muslims must show that critique is an essential part of the Quranic message, and that they are more open to critique and not afraid to express themselves freely or to be wrong, as errors are an essential part of learning.

The highest form of critique is self-critique, which consists of turning one's view inward before aiming a question outward. Of course, we believe that the Quran is the truth revealed through the Prophet. We hold it to be true, universal and infallible for all eternity. However, our interpretations are relative, impermanent, fallible. Our critiques, or self-critiques, target certain interpretations that some believers accept blindly, turning them into ideologues and self-proclaimed possessors of 'the' truth. Our approach claims to critique the dogmatic interpretations of the Quran as well as reactionary cultural traditions and customs. Some are good, others are not.

In this way, we challenge those in our generation who feel morally superior to others because they are Muslim and use the derogatory term *kafir* (plural *kuffar*), or unbeliever, to define all non-Muslims as equal to 'miscreants', 'ingrates' and 'infidels'. Equally contestable are Muslims who discourage young people from participating in the political sphere and, more generally, tell them to cut themselves off from Western society. In the same way, we critique the far right, which demonises Islam and Danish Muslims in the naïve hope that they will stop believing that the Quran is the revealed word of God. In this sense, the Forum for Critical Muslims sets itself up as an alternative to the Danish far right and the far-left Islamist groups who have one point in common: both want to make people believe that Islam and democracy are incompatible. 'We want to do away with the growing Islamophobia within the far right just as we want to knock down the iron curtain that some build between Islam and the West', our manifesto reads under the heading of 'Critique', its third pillar. 'We are fighting this battle with well-supported arguments, based on facts, qualified with the aid of balanced messages.'

Finally, 'multiplicity' makes up our fourth and last principle. The Quran proposes a complex, multifaceted, multiplicitous religious truth. In fact, no one can claim to be the owner of the community of Danish Muslims. Anti-representation is a keyword and our point of departure: no one can claim to speak in the name of Islam. Muslims express themselves in their own names. All attempts at grouping together Danish Muslims as a single entity have led to unending debates about who the 'real Muslims' are. By acknowledging multiplicity, we avoid these vain quarrels about 'authentic' Muslims. The idea that there is just one version or interpretation of Islam excludes those who stray from what is deemed the 'correct' version. People who neither accept nor tolerate diversity within Islam do not understand the texts and are causing divisions in society. It's not our different approaches to the Quran that divide society, but the negation of each person's right to defend their diverse views and interpretations.

According to the Quran, multiplicity and diversity are a blessing from God. The Quranic ideal of the good and just person is not defined by race, nationality, gender or belief. The only thing that distinguishes one human being from another is a person's spirituality, virtue, goodness and actions. Doing good around you and accepting your neighbour in spite of differences. Goodness, patience, mercy and a spirit of tolerance are the signs by which one can recognise those who carry Islam in their hearts. God created a multiple and diverse world because he wanted us to aspire to diversity, given that this multiplicity converges towards unity (*tawhid*) as personified in the Prophet Muhammad.

Based on these principles – four articles that form a sort of constitution – the Forum for Critical Muslims opens its doors. That very month, on 11 September, not long after lunch, I find myself at my parents' house in the suburbs of Copenhagen. We learn from the news that an aeroplane has just embedded itself in one of the towers of the World Trade Centre. We turn on the television and, in a daze, watch the live 'spectacle' of the second plane ploughing into the South Tower. We hold our breath as the presenter announces that two other planes have crashed, one into the Pentagon, in Washington, D.C., the other – United Airlines Flight 93 – in a field in the state of Pennsylvania, after some heroic passengers deliberately brought it to the ground while trying to regain control. The public discovers the terrorist organisation al-Qaeda and encounters the face of Osama bin Laden. Fear settles in. The atmosphere grows tense. Islam is often perceived as 'the' threat; Islamophobia is expressed without restraint. Because of these hundreds of fanatics – who will become thousands – Muslims in general are suspected of being radical Islamists and are called to justify themselves.

As a Muslim leader I feel that I have a responsibility to condemn these actions of terror but I'm aware that Muslims in general do not have a responsibility just because they are Muslims. Being active in the public sphere, I feel obliged to speak up. The brothers or the cousins of murderers are not responsible for their relatives' deadly acts: they are therefore not expected to provide an explanation for crimes they did not commit. In contrast, there is something insulting in these demands that each and every Muslim condemn the terrorists. Muslims are reproached for not producing a declaration of condemnation, but this ignores the fact that there are so many different voices within Islam ...

While I was hoping to improve our compatriots' view of Islam, the Forum for Critical Muslims is now beset by strong criticism from the far right. We struggle to defend ourselves, and the attacks only increase, criticising us for who we are. All the association members devote their energy to defending our mere right to be Muslim. The initial ambition of the Forum is put between parentheses. At the same time, as the Muslim question becomes headline news, my opinions are solicited more and more. I gain a certain notoriety as a regular debater on television in a climate increasingly marked by Islamophobia. On the shows in which I participate, it's not unusual for opponents to speak to me as though I'm an Islamist disguised as a moderate Muslim.

This feeling of injustice leads me to an irritating realisation. Certain parts of Western society have selective outrage, in spite of the universal values they display and claim. The question still irks me today. Why did the massacre of Srebrenica and the 8,000 killed not provoke the same emotion? During the American embargo against Iraq under the Clinton presidency, which caused the deaths of thousands of innocent Iraqi children, the world remained silent. Why? Who determines the number of victims at which the world should mobilise itself? There are so many events like 9/11 that have left the world indifferent: Srebrenica 1995, but also Gaza, where the only Israeli attack in 2014 caused 2,000 deaths in two months, of which three-quarters were civilians and innumerable children. Are the lives of Palestinians worth less than those of Americans?

I'm not trying to minimise the massacre of 9/11, but rather draw attention to the fact that, if official history is written by the victors, a large part of humanity perceives things differently. The new generation of Muslim Danes have a double imagination, even a double loyalty concerning the country their parents came from and the country in which they were born, and they should not be criticised for it. It's like being French-American. A part of your being, your memories, your imagination is French; the other is American. This is the case for me. I am Danish, and I am capable of making the mental leap that allows me to look at the world from Damascus and perceive things with a flexible global mentality. We are in the presence of a new globalised generation, tied to multiple loyalties, defying national borders. Yet a number of terrorists justify their acts precisely by the fact that in the eyes of the media some lives are apparently worth more than others. I'll say it again: it's not about trivialising 9/11, or minimising it (which would return to insulting the dead), but simply asking honestly why the deaths of 500,000 innocent people in Syria generates less empathy than 3,000 in New York?

Muslims are no more responsible for the World Trade Centre deaths than Christians are for the massacre of Utøya in Norway perpetrated by Anders Breivik in 2011, or than Jews are for the bombing of Gaza by the Israeli government in

2014 that killed more than 500 children in just a few weeks? In the little town of Dragør where I live, my daughter Aisha was the only Muslim in her class after the Paris attacks in 2015. She went to school the next day with a heavy heart. She told me she felt terrible in class because a classmate had asked the teacher why the attackers were always Muslim. The whole class turned to look at my daughter. A lot of Muslims feel this weight, the permanent injunction to take a position against terrorism. As though mass murder could provide such inspiration! Fortunately, Aisha's teacher was smart. She explained to the class that terrorism doesn't have a face, a name, a culture, a nationality or a religion, but that it's an awful political method that uses innocent lives without any regard for humanity. She added that it can happen in any context, including in Scandinavia, using the example of Anders Breivik, who justified the killing of seventy-seven young social democratic activists in the name of a 'modern Christian crusade'. According to Breivik, nostalgic for Nazism, social democrats threaten Christian order because they are 'agents of promotion' at the service of 'a multicultural society and thereby Islam'. But even though my daughter, like many others, can rationally detach herself from the feelings of guilt, her heart was still unsure about it, which made her sad.

A departure point for so many colonial wars and the theatre of so much mass violence – starting with the extermination of Jews in Europe – the West puts up with its own demons with good conscience, approaching indifference. At Mariam Mosque, an artwork made of embroidered fabric occupies an entire wall of the dining area, adjacent to the prayer room. The naïve work, made in the workshop of an artisan from the southern United States, depicts Mahatma Gandhi as a reporter holds a microphone out to him. The scene is authentic, and the dialogue that accompanies it, depicted in speech bubbles, defines the Western superiority complex. The reporter asks Gandhi: 'What do you think of Western civilisation?' And he gives this cutting reply: 'I think it would be a good idea.'

Seventy years after the assassination of the Hindu spiritual guide (Gandhi was killed by a Hindu fanatic), the West's defiance towards the rest of the world persists. Today, it has taken a new form called 'Islamophobia'. But, like the 'critical Muslims' of the past, Mariam Mosque proposes an alternative to the Islamists and the traditionalists in the media. Which kills two birds with one stone. Because it is also the most effective way to defuse Islamophobia.

Our approach does not consist of attacking the Islamist positions head-on because, *de facto* and whether or not we desire it, they are attracting a number of Muslims. We have to admit that, in European countries, political Islam is a fact. It's therefore up to us to offer powerful alternatives. Mine consists of delivering a critique of Islamism and peacefully addressing divisive topics. We have to find a way to study dangerous topics in a less dangerous way. I nuance the debate. Is Islamism described as the great enemy of Western democracy? Its existence is indeed problematic and must be challenged intellectually. But let us remember that Islamism is not a singular whole; it is polymorphous. It is sometimes expressed within the socialist movement, sometimes by the Sufi path, the radical movement, the reformist movement or even the jihadist movement. These are all very different things. Proclaiming that all of Islamic fundamentalism constitutes a threat serves no purpose. Some forms of Islamism are dangerous, others are not. For example, saying that Ennahda ('Renaissance Party'), the Tunisian Islamic political party, is equal to the jihadist Islamism of the ISIS militants makes no sense. We must propose an alternative discourse to that offered by radical Islamists. We must promote a tolerant Islam and spread progressive Islamic values. In this regard, Islamic feminism and Sufism are without a doubt some of the most powerful tools available to us.

CHAPTER FIVE

Balancing on a tightrope

Somewhere beyond right and wrong, there is a garden.
I will meet you there.

Rumi (1207–1273)

Ibn Arabi, the Islamic Sufi master and theologian (1165–1240), once said: 'the perfect man is a woman'. This is also typical of something my father would say. He is the first feminist I knew, as well as the first political activist, with a social democratic leaning to boot. He is one of my role models. He gave me his sense of political activism and his taste for current events and debating ideas. From my mother I inherited a taste for reading and contemplation and a philosophy of freedom. My parents, though protective, always wanted me to be independent and autonomous. But I also share a strong bond with my father, which reflects the paradox of wanting to both be free and belong. As a child, teenager and an adult, I have always felt free in their watchful eyes. Free to play outside after school with my friends in the neighbourhood, free to take the bus alone from the age of twelve, free to act in the theatre, take dancing lessons, choose my religion. Free to travel alone to London, Rome, Germany, Egypt and Syria, free to find my own partner and my own path. Their support has always been with me. When I was choosing what to study, when I left the family home, when I first began my political engagements, when I married a Danish man with Pakistani roots and when I decided to take the title of imam. My parents are educators of freedom.

After 9/11, Denmark sees a boost in populist fervour, as foreseeable as it is worrying. At the time, there is no doubt in my 'critical Muslim' mind: it's time for me to descend into the political arena in order to better fight for my ideas. Since the attacks in New York, the whole Western world, including Denmark, has started speaking in a loop about 'identity', 'values' and the 'clash of civilisations'. Islam, Islamists and terrorists are headline news almost every week. The editorialists dwell on the same subject: is Islam compatible with democracy? That's the big question. In spite of the scorn suffered by my community in the days following the attacks on the World Trade Centre, I am convinced that being both a practising Muslim and a fervent democrat obliges me to take a stand. I join Radikale Venstre, the Danish Social Liberal Party, one of the smaller parties that regularly participates in government coalitions, at least when the social democrats are in power.

In Danish 'Radikale Venstre' means 'Radical Left', but this party, whose audience oscillates between 5 and 10 per cent of voters, situates itself at the centre. Supported by my father, who is delighted to see his daughter following his political choices, I become a member of the party, preceded by my reputation as an activist. People now recognise the founder and leader of the 'critical Muslims'. My partisan rallying attracts the attention of the media, those lovers of 'good stories'. And mine *is* one, since I bring together ingredients that are contradictory in their eyes: practising Muslim and Danish democrat. On campaign platforms, as on television sets, I make a stand for Islam and refute Samuel Huntington's nebulous concept of the 'clash of civilisations', which is very much in vogue. It's seen as a good thing to speak about the necessity of establishing a dialogue between civilisations, an idea which I oppose. There is no so-called 'Islamic civilisation' or 'Western civilisation'; one cannot speak of the 'Muslim world' or the 'Western world' as a whole. I believe there is *one* civilisation, and within that civilisation we find different people with different ideas. The clash is therefore not between two civilisations but within the same civilisation, between dissimilar people with dissimilar ideas. Equality, tolerance, the rights of men and women, social solidarity and democracy are universal; such values are not the privilege of a geographic, cultural or religious space. Once again, the brilliant irony of Mahatma Gandhi according to which Western civilisation 'would be a good idea' comes to mind. No, the West does not have a monopoly on good feelings, justice and equality.

Starting in 2002, emboldened by my notoriety, I'm asked by party members to position myself to run for the legislative elections. Discovering the back kitchens of the political sphere, with all its calculations, manoeuvres and low blows, I quickly become disillusioned by the politics of politicians. At the time, international opinion is troubled over a distressing matter concerning stoning in Nigeria. A mother of thirty-one, Amina Lawal, has been condemned to death for adultery. The decision will be annulled the following year by the Sharia Court of Appeal in Katsina (in the north of the country). At the Danish Social Liberal Party's annual congress, happening at the same time, a party member (who is moreover not fond of me, as I threaten their political position) picks up on the story and, even though the subject doesn't appear on the day's agenda or in the debate schedule, they introduce a resolution titled 'No to Sharia Laws' that will be submitted to a delegates vote. They are hoping to profit from the condemnation of the unfortunate Amina Lawal, whose story is understandably troubling and tragic. As a sociologist of religions, I cannot subscribe to the erroneous representation of sharia as the one proposed by this politician with their limited understanding of Islam.

Sharia stems from the Quran and is central in Islamic faith, indicating to Muslims the way towards learning the mercy and knowledge of God. Sharia contains the five pillars of Islam, and it teaches Muslims how to live each day. It is important to differentiate between sharia and *fiqh*: sharia corresponds to the instructions given by God in the Quran, whereas *fiqh*, a fundamental notion in Islam, is the temporal interpretation of these instructions, or Islamic jurisprudence. However, it's essential to combine God's instructions and Islamic jurisprudence in a dynamic manner to find satisfying answers to the questions believers ask themselves.

On its own, reading the Quran is not enough. Believing in this sacred text as the expression of the word of God does not exclude common sense, criticism and the search for new knowledge. The greatest Muslim scholars consider most of the verses of the Quran and the teachings of the Prophet to be 'dynamic'; that is, that they must be reflected on by the ulama (scholars of Islam) or the muftis (legal scholars), along with Muslim legal experts, who are justified to educate believers concerning the nature of this or that action (licit, illicit or reprobate). The Quran in itself must not be read as a definitive, all-encompassing code of law. Combined with the Hadiths, the collection of the Prophet's oral traditions as reported by his companions, it sets the basis for the universal rules of conduct – ethical, spiritual and political – to be applied in modern society.

The principles of Islamic law are not fixed. They are general indications left to human intelligence to understand and apply in the community's best interests. It is up to humans to grab hold of their destiny and choose – in accordance with the eternal principles of Islam – the form of government best adapted to the reality of the moment. Just like the Decalogue, that is, the Ten Commandments, sharia sets down general principles. Some Muslims read them literally and some, as metaphors. I belong to the latter.

The negative reputation of sharia stems from the way in which certain people, groups and pseudo-Islamist states use and twist it for political ends. Their perverted practice of sharia should in no way be taken into account. In Denmark, some politicians and so-called experts of Islam are requiring Muslims to abandon sharia, the legal text and code of conduct. They argue that in order to belong to the Danish or European society one must renounce sharia. By making belonging dependent on renouncing the very core of Islam – the Quran as the revealed word of God – these politicians are, in effect, helping to marginalise and exclude the Muslim communities in their midst.

Being a 'secular Muslim believer' has nothing contradictory about it. Secularism does not signify non-religiosity, and religious legal arguments are acceptable as long as they don't aim at obtaining a particular statute or claiming political primacy. Secularism sets itself up as a barrier against all forms of dogmatism. It's against entrusting the church with political power. For all that, religion should not be banned from the public sphere or debate.

Distancing oneself from Islamic law, or sharia, in the way it is practised, for example, in Sudan, Iran, Saudi Arabia or Nigeria, is easy for European Muslims, and indeed Muslims in general, who reject the warped leaders of these nations. This should reassure all the pseudo experts of Islam and the worried Islamophobic politicians. But no: they want, it seems, to force Muslims to renounce the concept of sharia in general – which, I repeat, is equivalent to demanding that Jews and Christians abandon the Ten Commandments. Unlike such an approach, I am convinced it would be better to bring back the true meaning of sharia from a theological and etymological point of view, which is that of mercy and equality.

Let us add, to return to Amina Lawal, that stoning is not even mentioned in the Quran – stoning is only mentioned in relation to the stoning of Satan or the stoning against the newly converted Muslims. In fact, the penalty prescribed for the crime of adultery is neither death nor stoning, but one hundred lashes. According to some Muslim scholars, we must recall the time when this law was established and specify, of course, that this punishment applies (for both men and women) only in cases in which the adulterer or adulteress is a repeat offender and four eyewitnesses were present at the moment of the act. It is nearly impossible to meet these requirements, Muslim scholars would claim. What's more, it is enough for the offender to implore God four times in order to be absolved. And that's not all! If one of the four witnesses does not confirm the authenticity of the adultery, then the three others will be punished with eighty lashes 'for having dishonoured the reputation of a man or a woman'. In brief, this 'anti-adultery' law is to some Muslims above all a metaphor whose purpose is to show believers that lying is prohibited and adultery is not recommended. Many Muslims read this verse metaphorically, not literally. As for me, I'm against the death penalty and any kind of barbaric punishment, including lashes. The verse is not relevant to me in my understanding and interpretation of Islam, whether it is translated literary or metaphorically. The same reasoning goes for the penalty for stealing. It's not about cutting off a thief's hands. Because no Muslim endowed with common sense reads the passages concerning stealing in a literal manner. Reading the Quran must be put back in its historical context, interpreted with a critical consciousness and applied with solid theological knowledge. Consequently, the notion according to which 'the man is above the woman' should in fact only be understood in the sense that the man must protect his wife, not dominate over her.

In reality, sharia is compatible with European legislation. It already coexists with it, when Danish Muslims give alms (humanitarian work), pray, fast or marry. Islamic marriage therefore exists in parallel to civil marriage celebrated at the town hall. Evidently, the latter possesses the strength of law and prevails from an official and administrative point of view; but from a spiritual, religious and psychological point of view, it is the Islamic marriage that is the determining factor for practising Muslims.

Another example: Allah authorises commerce, but not lending with interest. God thus means to eradicate usury and develop the practice of charity. Islamic banks demonstrate to what point the principles, or laws, or sharia, are compatible with European legislation. Islamic banks are present, among others, in Malaysia, the United Arab Emirates, Pakistan, Bangladesh and Saudi Arabia, but also the United Kingdom. HSBC, the fourth-largest bank in the world, started a worldwide Islamic finance network, Amanah, some twenty years ago.

In sum, sharia, or the Islamic system of law and guidance, stems from the Quran and designates 'the path' or 'the way' of access towards respecting divine law. It offers a code of conduct that determines the laws as well as the individual and collective duties of Muslims, establishing a group of rules, prohibitions and sanctions for them. A large number of aspects of a Muslim's life are inspired by sharia: dietary restrictions, dress code, financial transactions, family rights, penal infractions, judiciary matters. But in no case does sharia recommend the stoning of women, contrary to the media's false presentation of it.

At the Danish Social Liberal Party's annual congress, the article on sharia law, motivated by the life-threatening and heartbreaking situation of Amina Lawal, is introduced not long before the party's vote on the final resolution. When the time comes to vote, the amendment is adopted by 698 votes. There were two dissenting votes. Mine was one of them. In the months that follow the trauma of 9/11, knowledge, sound arguments and reasoning are nothing in the face of fear, emotions and irrationality.

When I get home, a journalist from an influential tabloid calls me and asks: 'Do you confirm that you are an extremist in favour of stoning?' Cornered and accused, I am unable to get my knowledge across. In the following weeks, I am criticised and slandered by politicians in my own political party. My reputation is ruined.

The party demands that I give a speech to defend my position on the matter. After the speech, they will decide my fate. The Vartov conference centre, where I usually hold my conferences and seminars, is packed with hundreds of people from my party, as well as journalists who are eager to see whether the party will denounce their Muslim candidate for Parliament. From this day onwards, I'm referred to as the 'Muslim candidate' and not as Sherin Khankan, the influential activist. I climb up on to the stage to re-establish a few elements of this debate in which each person, overpowered by emotions, has been pretending to be an expert. In my speech, I explain why it would be right to refuse this anti-sharia article, as it is equal to mixing the barbarianism of the legal and political system in northern Nigeria with Islam in general. In my eyes, it is unacceptable. I also explain why I voted against the resolution. I recall to the assembly that stoning is not part of the Quran or sharia; that the countries which encourage it, Nigeria and Iran, are run by politicians who are corrupt, misguided, aggressive and abusive; and, like Amnesty International, we must condemn this barbaric practice, without falling into the trap of demonising the Quran and Muslims, paving the way for the far right. On this day, I win the battle: the content of the resolution is changed based on my critique. A new version of the text states that the Danish Social Liberal Party is against all barbaric forms of punishment, regardless of the way they are legislated.

Of course, some members of the party are not happy with this outcome, and they assume that, with a rival out of contention, their ascension to the candidacy will be easier. In fact, the candidacy I was seeking slips away from me. Determined to clear my name, I intend to take my slanderers to court. A bit disoriented, I go to my parents' house one evening to see my father. As he so often does, he offers me wise counsel: 'Why throw yourself into a fight that will be exhausting and in vain?' he says soothingly while serving me mint tea. 'You should instead devote yourself to what matters to you: the fight for women's rights and a newborn feminism within Islam.' I listen to him and decide to pull away from political involvement.

This ephemeral political career nevertheless allowed me to meet the future father of my four children. In 2002, while giving a speech on the theme 'Islam and democracy' at Christiansborg Palace (the seat of the Danish parliament), a young medical student introduces himself after my presentation. He is radiant, different from the people I've met up to now, glowing with a weighty intensity and sincerity that moves me, even though he is only twenty-two years old. A very handsome man and a Muslim, he tells me that his family is from Pakistan and that, like me, he was born and brought up in Denmark. I'm meeting him for the first time, but I already have a feeling I will spend my life with him. Later, he will confess to me that, during my speech, he leaned over to a Muslim brother and friend and whispered: 'That woman, Sherin, I'm going to marry her ... '

As I cycle home after the conference with my sister Nathalie, I repeat his name loudly with a smile. I tell my sister that if I ever have a boy, I'll name him after this man. (Four years later, I would have my second child, my first boy, and I indeed named him after him.) We see each other months later by accident at a conference at Copenhagen University. He then asks me out for an afternoon in Malmö, Sweden, thirty minutes by train from Copenhagen over the Øresund Bridge, which spans the strait known as the Sound. We have dinner and as if it were the most natural thing in the world, we plan our future together right there on our first date, without knowing each other. We are eager to make our connection official because we both dismiss the idea of living together before being officially united. This is my romantic side, seeking the absolute and somehow repeating my parents' story.

We are absolute opposites and have very different interpretations of Islam. I'm a Muslim on the spiritual Sufi path, while he's a politically-oriented Muslim dreaming of a revolutionary, united Muslim world based on equality and human rights. Everyone around us opposes the marriage, especially his relatives, since he is the first child in the family to break the tradition of Pakistanis only marrying Pakistanis. This is the classical dilemma of our time. Some of the older members of the second generation of immigrants and Muslims are 'slaves' to their national tribal identity, and so they seek to marry their children within the same tribes that they belong to. In doing so, they ignore the fact that Islam and the Prophet Muhammad recommended that Muslims marry across nations and tribes, and that Ali, the fourth caliph of Islam, said: 'Parents, you must teach your children something new every day. Something your parents did not teach you.'

I am even more attracted to him when, in asking me to marry him, he says: 'If, one day, your parents are having difficulties, we can take them in with us.' What young man, in our time, would think about my parents' needs before thinking of mine? I realise that, besides being romantic, he is serious as well and cares about planning for the future – two cardinal virtues in my eyes. My father's reaction is hardly encouraging: as a Syrian, he considers Pakistanis to be too conservative and traditional. He makes generalisations out of worry for his feminist daughter: 'A Pakistani? But it's the Middle Ages in their country!' Registering my determination, he changes his mind. And, as usual, my father envelops me with his benevolence and, after a time, warmly receives his future son-in-law, the father of our four children to come, when the latter goes to ask him for my hand in marriage. However, my future husband's family is hardly any more enthusiastic, saddened that their son is marrying a non-Pakistani. For the first time in my life, I discover the meaning of 'patriarchal structures'. Pakistan ... a universe opens up to me and I discover it, imagining the lyrics of a song by the Danish poet Benny Andersen: 'You kiss a mouth and marry a people'. In marrying my husband, I discover a new culture and a people I knew nothing about. And when you marry someone, it is surely not an individual act, because you marry the family, its traditions and its culture.

Four months after our date in Malmö, on 26 June 2003, we are married, first in a religious ceremony, then later that year on 20 September civilly. Contrary to the traditional Pakistani rites uniting remote families, we are married in reduced company. Our festivities are very much inspired by Sufi traditions, with a focus on simplicity and intimacy, with my new husband wearing a white cotton tunic over puffy pants and a long jacket, while I am dressed in a long white dress with a lightweight green veil pinned in my hair that falls down my back. We borrow from some Pakistani traditions but do not follow all the stages, as marriage ceremonies normally last for four days. According to tradition, the couple being married do not see each other between the first day and the fourth, the actual day of the marriage. The second is reserved for dancing; on the next day, the guests and the bride all wear red to pay honour to the banquet given by her family; and finally the ceremony concludes with a party. We come up with a condensed version of this protocol resembling the various stages in a single day. Our religious ceremony (following the Islamic marriage called *nikah*) is strange and conservative, led by a Syrian imam. To my surprise, I'm separated from my sister, mother and female cousins and friends during the Islamic marriage ritual performed by the Syrian imam in my parents' house. All the women have to wait in the house of my father's closest Syrian friend (I call him uncle) across the street while I'm left alone with all the men. While the ceremony isn't feminist, I am so in love that I make the best of it. If it had only been up to me, I would have planned our marriage ... in both a mosque and a Christian church, since I love the atmosphere in both houses of God. Since I believe our God is unique and common to us both, I think religious buildings should welcome marriages from the different monotheistic religions. I have a vision of building a house of prayer with three entrances and one big prayer room, uniting all three religions into one.

Our civil ceremony on 20 September is held at the Copenhagen town hall, a monumental building in the heart of the capital, right by Tivoli Gardens, in the large function room rented for a banquet for sixty guests. Later that day at the wedding reception, I take my father's arm as a Sufi brother recites verses from the Quran in song. I feel safe, since my husband and I are already married according to Islamic law and I now know him much better, having just returned from our honeymoon in Syria. Four years after the attacks in New York, while we are living the life of a young couple, busy raising our children, Denmark is the scene of a violent political crisis, with the so-called Muhammad cartoons controversy at its centre.

On 30 September 2005, the daily newspaper *Jyllands-Posten* publishes twelve editorial cartoons of the Prophet Muhammad. The images are the work of Scandinavian cartoonists, responding to a challenge from an editor at *Jyllands-Posten*, who invited artists to draw Muhammad as they perceived or imagined him. The drawings the newspaper received were not provocative enough, so they asked their own cartoonist for an illustration of the Prophet as well. *Jyllands-Posten*'s own cartoonist then drew a picture of a man wearing a turban in the shape of a bomb. In an article accompanying the drawings devoted to self-censorship and the freedom of the press, the newspaper claimed that freedom of speech in Europe was under threat, and that Muslims should learn to put up with being mocked and ridiculed, since this was a natural part of being Danish. Muslim tradition prohibits depictions of the Prophet, but Muhammad has nevertheless been portrayed in academic books throughout history without an outcry. However, the strong reactions have less to do with the Prophet being depicted than with the fact that he was depicted as a terrorist. Moreover, *Jyllands-Posten* is generally viewed as an anti-Islamic newspaper and has often depicted Muslims as problematic.

One of the twelve cartoonists breaks with the project, declaring the paper is only looking to promote controversy. Two weeks after the article's publication, several thousand Muslims demonstrate in Copenhagen. The next day, a young man is arrested in Aarhus – the country's second-largest city where the newspaper headquarters is located – for having issued death threats to two of the cartoonists. A few days later, eleven ambassadors from Muslim countries ask to be received by the Danish prime minister, who refuses. On 1 December, eight of the cartoonists and five representatives from the Muslim community meet confidentially. But the next day, an extremist group from Pakistan puts a price on the cartoonists' heads.

Between December and early January, a delegation of Danish imams travels to the Middle East to rally Muslim institutions and states. It's easy to understand that, feeling attacked, they resolve to defend themselves and show the twelve offensive drawings from *Jyllands-Posten*. Their tour gives an international dimension to the controversy. There are demonstrations in several countries and fires at several Danish embassies. At the end of January 2006, Syria calls on Denmark to punish those who target religion. Based in Cairo, the Federation of Arab Journalists denounces the spread of hate against Islam and Muslims. For his part, Mohammed Mahdi Akef, the head of the Muslim Brotherhood, a political movement in Egypt, tells Muslims around the world to boycott Danish products. This demand seems to me like an attempt to break the monopoly held by the producers of Western opinions. In other words, while a newspaper and twelve cartoonists decree that it is permissible to use mockery that is insulting to the Muslim faith in the right to inform, Muslim believers refuse to be mocked in such a way. I believe the steps taken by the newspaper were unhealthy in presenting the following murky equation: in order to see whether the Muslims in Denmark are really Danish, they joke, they need to accept our mockery, because then they're truly assimilated citizens. The arguments of the supporters of the so-called freedom of expression could be formulated in this way: 'With these drawings, we declare that Muslims are authentic Scandinavians, since those faithful to the Prophet have the right to the same treatment and the same mockery as anyone else.' This argument is problematic and manipulative. It seems to me that freedom of expression must be used more delicately. If someone makes fun of another person and humiliates them concerning a topic that is essential to their identity, their faith, their pride, where is the dialogue the mocker is claiming to establish?

On 1 February, the press takes up the twelve cartoons once more, in Flemish Belgium and Germany. In France, *Charlie Hebdo* publishes them on 8 February, adding other cartoons of Muhammad drawn by the magazine's regular contributors. In Denmark, tensions between communities worsen. The far-right Danish People's Party, which is hostile to immigrants, calls for a vote on the country's anti-immigration laws, considered the most restrictive in Europe, backed by its having 13 per cent of the seats in Parliament. According to a big name in the party who was formerly a preacher, 'Islam is not compatible with Danish traditions' because 'cartoons of Jesus are wholly tolerated in these traditions'. He claims that 'Muslims have come to Denmark to invade us, just as they have done for 1,400 years.' Louise Frevert, an MP from the Danish People's Party, goes even further, comparing Muslims to a 'cancerous tumour'.

For some Muslims, the debate over freedom of expression serves as a pretext for aggression, aiming to provoke reactions of identity and paving the way for the far right. In this tense climate, some young Danish Muslims on the defensive are seduced by the discourse of Hizb ut-Tahrir, an Islamist party that has turned Islam into a man-made political ideology and promotes 'pure Islamic doctrine, the Caliphate'. For the sake of appeasement, several Danish editorial writers denounce 'the toughening climate around Muslim immigrants'. One influential writer notes that, although 'some Muslims insist that special consideration be given to their own religious sentiments, it isn't necessary to ridicule them, hold them in contempt or make a mockery of them at all costs to verify the solidity of our secular democracy or our tradition of the freedom of expression'. At the same time, the president of the European Network Against Racism declares that 'it is not by chance that this controversy broke out in Denmark. No country in the European Union is more Islamophobic or xenophobic.'

We watch as a conflict builds, one that seeks to demonstrate the existence of an enemy from within, a fifth column. As a representative of the association of 'critical Muslims', I am solicited by the media. After the fire at the Danish embassy in Damascus, I feel the need to express myself and I call a meeting of the main representatives of Danish Muslim associations in order to try to extinguish this evil flame that was pointlessly lit by the *Jyllands-Posten* cartoonists. Our objective is to find a way to spread a message seeking to calm people's hearts that, coming from Danish Muslims, will have enough weight to reach the rest of the Islamic world. I personally never felt insulted by these cartoons because I don't see any relation between God, our beloved Prophet Muhammad and the bad drawings. But I do consider negatively stereotyping all Muslims as violent barbarians to be problematic and dangerous, preventing any dialogue from taking place. To draw a turban in the shape of a bomb is to declare that the whole of the Muslim community is warlike, and to blame it for the attacks and their victims.

As I watch the controversy, I think of the Prophet's voyages to Ta'if and his famous prayer of the same name. In 619, he walked to the city, located about seventy miles from Mecca. Greeted with insults, he declared: 'All that does not matter, as long as I do not incur Your anger, because, for me, Your favour is more vast than anything. I seek refuge in the light of Your Face by which You dispel the shadows and correct every affair of this world and hereafter, against any discharge of Your anger upon me. I seek nothing but to satisfy You and there is no power and no might except by You.' These words inspire me as I write a calming message to the Muslim world; they carry me as I participate in televised debates. Each time I insist on this peaceful idea, central to the Sufi spiritual approach. If the Prophet could endure being attacked and mocked in Ta'if, then we can put up with it, too.

Looking back, I haven't changed my mind: for me, the cartoons controversy has nothing to do with the freedom of expression. It cannot exempt itself from a sense of responsibility. Yet in the many years before the controversy, *Jyllands-Posten* denigrated Islam, making it appear ontologically negative. The freedom of expression must not be used to attack minorities but, much more, to defend them. As a very active participant in the debates, I stand firm on this position. But the debate is a trap. As soon as I offer any reasoning, explaining for example my reasons for opposing the cartoons on principle, everyone concludes, with syllogisms, that I am an adversary to the freedom of expression. However, there are two fundamental notions that are equally sacrosanct in my eyes: the sacred character of the Quran and the freedom of expression.

The debate over the *Jyllands-Posten* cartoons controversy can be viewed from three different perspectives. Some claim it represents a clash between the Islamic and Western civilisations. Others say it is about the unfettered right to free speech and artistic freedom. Finally, there are those who argue that it is the physical manifestation of Europe's right-wing politics and the belief, forged with the birth of Orientalism and embodied by the 9/11 attacks, that Islam is a threat. The cartoons controversy evoked such strong reactions from Muslims around the world because the drawings depicted Islam as a primitive, misogynistic and violent religion while casting its prophet in a negative light. They attacked what Muslims feel is the essential element at the heart of Islam: the belief that the Prophet was a merciful revolutionary who challenged all forms of discrimination, be it racial, national, social, religious or, not least, sexual. The Muslims' Prophet is the living symbol of all that is good and just, and he is the supreme role model for Muslims, just as Jesus is for Christians.

The cartoons also challenged the idea of the Quran as holy scripture. The sacredness of the Quran does not stem from some passive dogma, nor does it require that people refrain from taking an active, critical and interpretive approach towards its contents. Many modern scholars have, in fact, urged both men and women to interpret those passages of the Quran that are open to interpretation in the context of their own era and society. The Quran's sacred character comes from the deep sense of *adab* ('decorum' or 'respect') Muslims have for the Quran and the customs established by the Prophet Muhammad. *Adab*, which can also be translated as 'good manners', 'sensitivity' or 'propriety', is observed by active Muslims and many non-Muslims. And just as you don't have to be a Muslim to understand *adab*, you don't need to be a Muslim to express wildly irrational emotions about religion. In the 1970s, Danish artist and filmmaker Jens Jørgen Thorsen set off an international firestorm with his plans for a sarcastic film about Jesus. The pope condemned the project and the Danish embassy in Rome received bomb threats. The fact of the matter is that religion has always and everywhere been an emotional flashpoint.

The cartoons controversy illustrates the potential for conflict when one group has the right and power to define universal principles for all groups. The Western concept of globalisation, for example, is not the same as the Muslim conception of globalisation. For many practising Muslims, the idea that the Quran is sacred scripture is just as fundamental as freedom of speech is for those in the West. However, this isn't the same as saying that practising Muslims don't consider freedom of speech or a critical approach to religion to be important concepts. What often offends many Muslims about Western globalisation is that their religion is made relative. For some, compromising the Quran's sacredness at all is too high a price to pay to join the global community. Ironically, some Muslims reach the alternative conclusion that Islam and freedom of speech are incompatible, which is a win for the European far right, as well as for far-left Islamist groups that claim Islam and democracy are incompatible, since only God can create laws. As the West's monopolisation of values such as democracy and freedom of speech turns universals into something 'non-Islamic', we dig artificial divides between Islam and democracy, 'them' and 'us', faith and secular thought.

There are many Muslims, including me, who accept that there are different attitudes and interpretations of Islam and its message. But at the same time, we shouldn't give up the right to use well-reasoned arguments to combat all forms of hateful speech and propaganda disguised as 'art'. I am encouraged by non-Muslims who accept that some Muslims have a relative approach to freedom of speech, in which they can acknowledge the Quran as sacred while embracing freedom of speech. Being able to accept two universal principles at the same time is, in my view, essential. For Muslims, this means arguing that both principles are important and compatible. If Europeans and non-Muslims want to establish good relations with the new Middle East, Muslims in the West and indeed the Muslim world, they need to accept points of view that differ from their own and be aware that others can have different values and sensitivities from their own. The freedom of speech is not an unconditional right to say whatever you want – it is not the right to spew hateful propaganda.

Ultimately, I believe we should contest the *Jyllands-Posten* cartoons, but in a spirit of tolerance. This was the way the Prophet Muhammad reacted when he was subjected to hate, ridicule and physical assault. He sought not humanity's acceptance, only God's. Accordingly, the Quran tells us: 'But indeed if any show patience and forgive, that would truly be an exercise of courageous will and resolution in the conduct of affairs' (42:43).

A tragic extension of the cartoons controversy happened on 7 January 2015 with the terrorist attack against the French satirical magazine *Charlie Hebdo*, which had also published the *Jyllands-Posten* drawings of Muhammad years earlier.

Naturally, like the vast majority of Muslims, I don't consider the perpetrators of these heinous crimes to be Muslims. Such attacks and killings committed by terrorist organisations have no place in our religion. According to Islamic principles, 'whoever kills a person, it is as though he has killed all mankind. And whoever saves a life, it is as though he had saved all mankind.'

Unfortunately, cartoons, simplification, parody, aggression, violence and crime seem to have become the modes of communication of our time. By campaigning for feminism within Islam, developing the idea of a female imamate and promoting dialogue, openness and tolerance, our approach at Mariam Mosque has been to situate ourselves at the opposite end of such ways of behaving.

CHAPTER SIX

Looking at the future of Islam

Verily, Allah will not change the condition of a people until they change what is in themselves.

Quran Sura Ar-Ra'd 13:11 ('The Thunder')

In my home, I feel safe and sound. With four children, our house is rather animated, rarely calm, but I love the sound of children playing. My home decor combines the Nordic and Oriental styles. Hanging on the walls of the living room and kitchen are pictures of women in religious and revolutionary scenes, symbols of freedom. Apart from that, my home probably looks like those of most Danes: a functional kitchen, children's rooms cluttered with toys, light wooden furniture, lots of candles, a comfortable couch in the living room and a chaise longue in the library, where I've collected the books of Shakespeare, Jean-Paul Sartre, Søren Kierkegaard, Rumi, Ibn Arabi, Albert Camus, Haruki Murakami, Karen Blixen, Fyodor Dostoyevsky, Mahmoud Darwish, Shaykh Fadhlalla Haeri, Amina Wadud and Paulo Coelho, but also a large number of theological works and classics of Scandinavian theatre such as Ibsen and Strindberg, as well as the Finnish national epic, *The Kalevala*, to name but a few. Aside from a prayer mat, moved from the living room to my bedroom depending on the time of day, nothing suggests an imam lives here.

In 2007, we left our apartment in Copenhagen, which had become too small with two children, and moved south to the village of Dragør, in the suburbs of the capital, where the red and black brick buildings are replaced by individual houses painted yellow or white and surrounded by lush dark farmland. It takes about half an hour to reach Copenhagen's lively city centre by public transport. Three years ago, we found the house of our dreams, also located in Dragør. I immediately fell in love with this house and its romantic setting: a former manor home next to some farm buildings, in the middle of almost five acres of land.

A majestic gravel driveway separates the main gate, by the road, and the buildings, which surround a former courtyard on all sides. When I drive along this straight line, I always feel like I belong to the old days. However, I'm just one of several who live in this property, which has been divided into nine separate flats. Ours is located in the 'noble' part, that is, in the manor house – divided into three apartments – facing the driveway. The other flats are behind the house in the former barns and stables, now transformed into typical Danish apartments full of designer furniture and Lego. The neighbours are pleasant, with energetic children the same ages as my own who play football, cricket, with dolls and hide-and-seek together on the lawn. The children go from one house to another, meeting up to play, running around, shouting, making up imaginary games, bringing life to our community. After school, they play at each other's houses or on the huge shared lawn until evening. I don't even need to look at my watch to know it's almost 6 p.m. There's always one of my four children who runs up shouting: '*Mor, jeg er sulten!*' (Mum, I'm hungry!)

Our kitchen has a view of the courtyard. It connects to the dining room, which looks out on the other side of the house, towards the lawn, some big trees and the main driveway. The children's rooms and the laundry room are on the ground floor and our bedroom is upstairs. On the side facing the lawn, under the windows of the semidetached house next door, our now former neighbour, a quiet, heavyset man, set up a kennel for his two Dobermanns, with aluminium fencing six feet high. The set-up wasn't the most pleasing to look at and reminded me of the prison at Guantanamo. … On a regular basis, when I unrolled my mat in the living room for my prayers at noon (*dhuhr*), in the afternoon (*'asr*) or at sundown (*maghrib*), I used to see my neighbour feeding his dogs.

In the months preceding the opening of the mosque, my house became a hive of activity, the epicentre of 'a positive conspiracy' that consisted of promoting women's place within Islam. In the absence of a locale to accommodate a mosque, the preparatory meetings took place in my living room, where I also ended up officiating the mosque's first Islamic marriage. Our movement, Femimam, has several founding members, all remarkable individuals: Saliha Marie Fetteh, an expert in the Arabic language, and Saer El-Jaichi, who holds a PhD in Islamic philosophy and is an expert on Islam and a lecturer at Copenhagen University. We also have committee members from abroad, including a young Muslim woman named Mahvish Ahmad, who is a PhD student at Cambridge, as well as other Muslim scholars who support our cause. Our little group often meets at my house. We write memos, discuss theology and devise communication strategies. One of our debates centred on the question of gender diversity. Should we reserve access to our future mosque to women only, or allow the prayer room to be mixed gender? Personally, I leaned towards the latter option. But the majority were in favour of a 100 per cent female option and, after many discussions, I joined the majority. Our meetings were always interspersed with meals and prayers. Around 3 p.m., the children would come home from school, make noise, ask for a snack, come into the room, go out into the courtyard, then come back again, playing, arguing, shouting and laughing. It was quite like a caravanserai ... which was not at all to my former neighbour's liking when he was living next door.

One morning, when we both happened to be outside on our doorsteps, I approached my neighbour to ask him why he ostensibly ignored me while being friendly with the other neighbours. He explained that he didn't appreciate the comings and goings of all the women and journalists. 'I don't like it,' he said warily. 'I work for the Ministry of Defence and don't want to be associated with all that.' I then learned that the owner of the two Dobermanns once fought in Afghanistan. I tried to reassure him, guaranteeing that no photos would be taken, but he cut me short. Then he declared his dislike for fundamentalist Muslims. I responded that I'm on the Sufi path, and explained to him in broad strokes that Sufism is the spiritual path within Islam that seeks to unite people beyond their religious and ethnic differences. But I wasted my breath; with a scowl, the ex-soldier simply walked off towards the imposing metal structure of his kennel, accusing me and my family of being Muslim fundamentalists. For two years until he moved away, he refused to say hello or even look at me, other than the two times he shouted threats in my direction.

In our time, living out one's Muslim faith isn't easy in Western society. Since 9/11, the debate over Islam in Denmark can be characterised by arguments in the form of threats and claims like 'Islam is threatening Western democracies'. These forms of 'reasoning' rest on fears and emotions that are often unfounded and irrational. They tend to reverse and supplant any logic.

For the past ten years or so, the Muslim academic community has been buzzing. Subjects ranging from the rise of fundamentalism, the interpretation of sacred texts, the nebulous concept of the 'clash of civilisations', the political systems in the Middle East, or women's place in Islam are all at the heart of impassioned debates taking place around the world. At the same time, the Quran has become a 'bestseller' in Europe and the United States, with readers hoping to find answers to their questions. As for me, around the end of 2006, I discover the activism of Amina Wadud. A professor of Islamic studies at Virginia Commonwealth University, Amina converted to Islam in the 1970s and is a prominent figure in Muslim feminism. She was the first woman to give an introductory sermon (*khutbah*) in a mosque, which occurred in Cape Town, South Africa, in 1994. This scholarly woman, who was educated at American universities, was also bold enough to lead a mixed-gender Friday prayer (*salat*) at a mosque in New York in March 2005. This prayer, during which the women were not separated from the men, had already taken place when I learned about it. At the time, Wadud's prayer was announced in a press release on the internet, which referenced the Friday prayer led in Medina by Umm Waraqa, who was renowned for her capacity to recite the Quran in its entirety, and who led a Friday prayer in Medina with the authorisation of the Prophet – blessed may he be: 'A woman will deliver the *khutbah* and lead the prayer for a mixed-gender congregation. It will be the first public *Jum'ah* [Friday] prayer of its kind on record since Prophet Muhammad, upon whom be peace and blessings, reportedly authorized Umm Waraqa to lead her household in prayers[1]. ... It took us 1,400 years to do it again.

On the day of the prayer, Amina Wadud, dressed in a grey hijab, participated in a press conference before the occasion alongside several women organisers which explained the meaning of the event. One of the organisers, Asra Nomani, summarised the general state of mind: 'The voices of women have been silenced through centuries of man-made traditions, and we are saying, no more, enough is enough, we are going to take our rightful place in the Muslim world. We are reclaiming the place that the Prophet Muhammad and Islam gave us in the seventh century, and we are going to be part of the solution. ... We are going to be cities of light to the Muslim world so that all can follow this lead.'[2] A few hours earlier, Nomani, an American writer and activist of Indian origin, gave an interview on the Al Jazeera network, affirming, 'Today is the dawn of a new day in the history of Islam. We are opening the door of the Muslim world to women and to people of all faiths. This is not just about mosques, this is about our Muslim faiths, this is about our Muslim community. It is about opening up the doors of Islam to everyone. ... Americans and the West have to deal with glass ceilings; we have brick wall in front of us, and we are hammering them down.'[3]

When I later read those words, uttered in a city still suffering from the shock of the World Trade Centre attacks, a shiver went down my spine. Such words are as audacious as they are invaluable. The organisers of the prayer argued against the idea of gender segregation in mosques, in which women are generally separated from and relegated behind men, often in basements, entrances or even another room where the sermon is broadcast on loudspeakers. This practice is not prescribed by the Quran, but rather by a tradition based on the idea that men's minds are so corrupt that, if women are not hidden from view, they are incapable of concentrating on the prayer.

Copenhagen is at once a European capital and a village, as its modest size allows one to bump into acquaintances on a regular basis. In 2015, I meet up with my activist friend Mahvish Ahmad, a former member of the Forum for Critical Muslims, who has just returned from Lahore, Pakistan, where she lived and taught at a university for several years. We meet up in the evening and talk about the 'good old days' for several hours. We share our regrets, bringing up the memory of the time when the 'critical Muslims' were more active. 'It's too bad our organisation never became a mass movement, because we were disseminating important ideas,' she says. This sentence electrifies me. I later recall it as I review my life, collect my thoughts and draw up a list of my real passions. This appraisal leads me to two troubling conclusions: wherever I look, women are not being treated as men's equals; and Islamophobia is spreading around the world like wildfire. As a woman, a Muslim and a mother of four, including two girls, I am directly affected and decide to act, to change things, to fight. Sometimes, when a situation seems blocked at the individual level, you have to take things higher, to the collective, universal level, in order to pull apart its knots. Thinking big allows you to remove yourself from a situation and better reflect on it. In my mind, these thoughts converge into a slogan: women are the future of Islam. Some Muslims seem to have forgotten or neglected the fact that women at the time of the Prophet played a significant role in disseminating the Muslim faith. In the same tradition, Muslim women of today are reclaiming their place in Islam as they have always done.

Heading to Istanbul, where I will give a speech at an international conference on women in Islam, I meet Saliha Marie Fetteh, who converted to Islam several years ago. On the plane, we talk about this and that, and when I bring up the idea of founding Femimam, an association whose ultimate goal would be the creation of a mosque for women, she is filled with enthusiasm. As I do every time I travel somewhere for a conference, I always reserve a handful of hours to take in a few sights. Accompanied by Saliha and other members of the conference group, including imams from Denmark and the Middle East,

I visit the extraordinary Hagia Sophia (built under the Byzantine emperor Justinian I), then the no less sublime Blue Mosque right across from it. There, women cannot go through the main entrance, but must enter this holy place through a little door on the side. Once again I am troubled, inwardly perturbed and saddened by the fact that Islam, a religion of love and peace, practises such discrimination in the smallest details of daily life.

A few hours before climbing up on to the stage, I throw my speech in the bin and write a new one that includes the concept of 'women imams'. As I rewrite my text, I dwell on the expression 'power doesn't ask, it takes'. This is so true ... even if this notion is relative in so far as taking power requires at the very least the implicit agreement of the people who grant it to you. Before I get up to speak in front of an audience of activists, intellectuals and imams from fifteen different countries, I think about the fact that the potential existence of 'women imams' doesn't represent a challenge to Islam as much as it does a way to fight Islamophobia. If we can show that women are men's equals in mosques, then the racists and Islamophobes will be deprived of one of their favourite arguments ... Taking advantage of the presence of imams from all over the world at the conference, I test the idea of a mosque for women and perceive a certain amount of surprise in the auditorium. 'Interesting but strange, interesting but strange, interesting but strange,' an imam from the Middle East, seated in the front row, repeats three times into his beard.

Back in Copenhagen, my little tribe – my parents and four children – come to pick me up at the airport and celebrate my return as though I've been away for a month. Halima, the youngest, jumps on me at once. Salaheddin tells me about his day at school. Aisha and Djibril spontaneously decide to set the dinner table. What a privilege to feel so loved and supported. The next day, I get back to work. I contact Aminah Tønnsen, a Danish Muslim author known for her books that present a rereading of the Quran, and ask her if she would like to become one of the imams of the future Mariam Mosque. From the start, I imagine creating an institution that rests on the legitimacy of a collective of women. But she declines, explaining that her progressive engagement hasn't spared her family. She makes it clear that, after making a large contribution to a better understanding of Islam in Denmark through a spiritual approach to the religion, she's decided that it's now time to devote herself to her family. Consequently, I am forewarned of the impact opening a mosque for women could have on my personal and family life. ... Aminah Tønnsen advises me to recruit Saliha Marie Fetteh, with whom I've just had such a pleasant experience on the plane to Istanbul. With my intentions confirmed, I get in touch with Saliha. She agrees to join me on this adventure.

More and more, I realise that my life is going to change. To be sure, the religious label will never leave me, and I worry about how this will affect my family life. The title of 'imam' is one of the most notorious in Denmark at this moment. My husband likes the idea of a mosque for women. But at the same time, he is ambivalent – he doesn't like my being so involved in the project and becoming one of the women imams. My father feels the same way. As for my eldest daughter, Aisha, who always listens attentively to our adult conversations at dinner time, she understands that the stakes are high. One day, she asks me why I don't find a normal job rather than getting involved in the imamate by starting a mosque.

Should I force this on my children? The same evening after my conversation with Aminah Tønnsen, as I'm reading stories about Pippi Longstocking to my dear little girl Halima, these questions torment me. But once she is asleep, I choose to ignore my fears and run headlong towards the risks. I decide to take inspiration from the remarkable women around the world who have already started mosques with women imams officiating. I set myself into motion, take action and get to work. I focus on positive thoughts and feel strongly that the goal is within reach if I can manage to bring together a group of women who are ready to work and fight patriarchal structures. Not long afterwards, I start recruiting competent academics who specialise in the Arabic language, Sufism, Muslim philosophy, Islamic archeology and other related fields. Apart from one close friend, all the other members of the new Femimam movement are people whom I've never met before. One of them is a young man I met through a social network, where he arduously defends the Femimam project against all the Muslim critics – both men and women – who are opposed to the idea of a female imamate. He will become one of the driving forces of our project and its cofounder.

Around the same time as the creation of Femimam, I publish an article in the Danish daily newspaper *Politiken* – Denmark's equivalent of *The New York Times* in America or the *Guardian* in the United Kingdom – about the vision for the Mariam Mosque and the concept of women imams. Widely read and shared on social networks, the article creates ripples and provokes debate.

In any case, providence comes knocking at my door, or rather that of the Femimam association. In the spring of 2016, a call comes from the famous Danish photographer and activist Jacob Holdt, who tells me that his tenants have terminated their lease, and that he will soon be able to put at my disposal a property of over 800 square feet in the centre of the capital to accommodate Mariam Mosque. As I am on the underground, I try to mask my joy but can't stop repeating *Allahu Akbar* (God is great) and 'Oh thank you, Jacob, thank you!' over and over, to the amazement of the other passengers in the carriage … Here I thought I would be seeking funding for years, and I suddenly find myself with a key in hand to a mosque! I'm often asked: who pays for the mosque? The answer is simple. Jacob has given us use of the space, and the charges connected to the functioning of the mosque – electricity, maintenance, etc. – are paid for with the rents from three small NGOs that each occupy a modest office space within the mosque itself.

Three months later, once Jacob's place has been renovated and repainted, Mariam Mosque opens its doors. I also officiate at a marriage, my second after one that was organised at my home in Dragør. It is an interfaith marriage, between a young Swedish Christian man and a Swedish Muslim woman of Pakistani origin. The couple whom I married at my home a year before had come to us from Norway after being unable to find a single imam who would marry them in Europe, because the man was a Christian believer and the woman a practising Muslim. They came to me as soon as they heard about the approaching opening of Mariam Mosque. They wanted to get married without converting to one or the other's religion, because each was a steadfast believer in his or her own faith. The woman wanted to be married by an imam, since she considered it the only valid form of marriage. However, the young couple faced almost a hundred refusals, from ninety-six imams throughout Scandinavia and the rest of Europe. Coming from neighbouring Norway, they were relieved to learn that they hadn't made the trip for nothing when I confirmed to them – as I had already explained over the phone – that a marriage at Mariam Mosque would be perfectly feasible as long as the families on both sides agreed, the couple had a deep and mutual respect for each other, and they would be legally married under Norwegian law as well.

In looking at these two children of globalisation, I couldn't help thinking of my own parents' interfaith marriage, as well as my own, also based on such cultural mixing. Their situation illustrates a scenario that is becoming more and more common in Europe. A growing number of Muslim women are choosing non-Muslim men, often Christians, as their life partners of choice. As imams and people in charge of Islamic spiritual care, my colleagues and I must find new responses to this situation, which is presenting today's young people with considerable dilemmas.

The marriage preparations consist of a series of preliminary interviews meant to understand the couple's situation, verify the sincerity of their choice and guide them in their spiritual journey as a married couple. When I welcome a couple into Mariam Mosque for the first time, we serve them some tea and cake. We light the candles in the chandelier to create a peaceful atmosphere and put the young couple at ease. For two hours, I explain the marriage proceedings and the implications of such a union. We also discuss their respective family environments. In some cases, I can sense some worry starting to show at this point. Some couples are afraid of facing their parents' reluctance. In the framework of an Islamic marriage, approval from the bride's family is preferred. If the parents refuse to give their children their approval due to race, nationality or religion, I try to bring about reconciliation. But in the end, the couple has the 'Islamic' right to marry. No matter what happens, I always advise the couple to try to obtain their parents' consent. This is preferable, and in fact goes for all marriages, Islamic or otherwise.

In one year, the mosque has hosted thirteen weddings. Some involve young men who convert to Islam before getting married, whereas others, with the blessing of Mariam Mosque, enter interfaith marriages. When couples arrive at Mariam Mosque, accompanied by their parents and witnesses, I'm always as overcome with emotion as they are. After taking off their shoes, the couple and those with them enter the prayer hall where the ceremony will take place. In general, some of the members of the mosque are also present. The couple sit on big dark-green cushions, the colour of hope, which is also associated with Islam in general. Their parents sit on either side of the couple and the rest of those in attendance sit behind them. Everyone is turned towards Mecca.

I start by reciting a *sura* from the Quran, then I give a *du'a* (an invocation to God). After this, I give a sermon of around twenty minutes based on my conversations with the couple: why they chose each other, etc. This includes stories from the Quran, extracts from the life of the Prophet – blessed may he be – as well as reflections on marriage and the art of loving each other. I often emphasise that a marriage is not just the partnership of two lovers, but also a union of two families, two cultures, two nationalities and, in the case of interfaith marriages, two religions. It is also a small but crucial contribution to the unity of humanity. Marriage is among the most intimate forms of friendship, in addition to being one of the most challenging on a daily basis. It is often described as a test of endurance in the face of God in order that God can know us. As for me, I see it as a test designed to ensure that we know ourselves and each other. If we hurt each other, we must seek forgiveness from our partner, not from God. The path to Allah is revealed to us in our encounters with our human brothers and sisters and in the discovery of ourselves. When we hurt someone, we hurt ourselves. I repeat before all in attendance that marriage concerns our ability to persevere; that it requires courage, tears and willpower, even when all seems lost. The perfect union is an illusion. In reality, marriage requires patience – above all, patience with our partner's weaknesses and our own. It is an effort that mobilises a deep inner love regarding the weaknesses of the other.

After my sermon, I proceed with the Islamic rituals: the couple mutually agree to take each other by saying 'yes', then we sign the *nikah* (marriage) contract. At the moment of signing, everyone sits in a half circle around the couple. It is essential to have the agreement of the bride and groom and of their parents. I should specify that forced marriages, which are common in some rural areas of Muslim countries, do not stem from Islam but from a traditional practice that I – along with the majority of Muslims – condemn.

Also required are the presence of witnesses and the groom's solemn request to the bride's parents for their daughter's hand. As for the dowry, which is also part of the tradition, it isn't the groom's way of buying a wife, but of expressing his love for her according to his means. Most of the time, the young couples at whose marriages I officiate do not interpret the requirement of the *mahr* (dowry) literally, but as something symbolic. For them – and they are not wrong – a ring can suffice. Thinking back on my own marriage, I thought that the wedding ring was enough. But the Syrian imam then audibly explained to my father that the price of the *mahr* had to be particularly high in cases of intercultural marriages because the risk of their failing was unusually elevated. After the signing of the contract, everyone gets up and surrounds the young couple. We recite the *shahada* (the Islamic declaration of faith) and the Al-Fatihah sura ('The Opening'), the first in the Quran, and then the marriage is official.

In the first weeks following the opening of Mariam Mosque, we keep a low profile and maintain a certain amount of discretion regarding our address so that we don't find ourselves drowning in media solicitations. At the Friday prayer, our doors remain closed, in order to preserve the spirituality of the moment and to protect the participants. Yes, we meet a certain amount of resistance from the Muslim community, but that's entirely normal in so far as we're beginning to question the masculine monopoly and patriarchal structures within Islamic institutions. As the first mosque in Scandinavia with women imams, we are writing a new page in the story of female Muslim leadership in religious institutions. But the opposition we meet is moderate and examples thereof are limited in number. I have not received any threats. When I speak in public, I always emphasise the positive aspects of our actions and support; this reinforces our legitimacy and makes it easier for others to support *us*.

The criticism we face focuses on the question of our legitimacy. Our opponents continuously ask me questions like: 'Does this mosque have the right to be here? Is it an authentic mosque? Are you a real imam?' In sum, people want to know if Denmark's first mosque for women and its religious leaders are truly legitimate in exercising their functions. Our legitimacy is based on three elements: theology, the needs (or requests) of believers and, finally, our experience and knowledge.

The first point, theology, is fundamental. The existence of a mosque for women is part of Islamic tradition. It may not be the most widespread, but it exists. Mariam Mosque is not an invention claiming to be some kind of reform. On the contrary, we are going back to the roots of Islam. What does the Quran say about women imams? Nothing. But it notes that women are men's equals and their partners on a spiritual, intellectual and social level. Like men, women are expected to seek and disseminate their knowledge. We must therefore look for an answer concerning women imams in the Hadiths, the oral accounts written down two centuries after the Prophet's death that relate his words and actions. The Hadiths report that after fleeing Mecca for Medina, the Prophet set up a mosque in his house where two women would lead the prayers. One was Aisha, his third wife, and the other was Umm Salama, his sixth. Muhammad's house was the first mosque in Islamic tradition and history. And this mosque accommodated women imams with the blessing of the Prophet himself.

One Hadith specifies that the Prophet Muhammad also sought out Umm Waraqa, the woman renowned for her capacity to recite the entire Quran, in order to entrust her with the task of leading prayer for her community – an assembly of both men and women. This episode is reported in the famous *Kitab al-Tabaqat Al-Kabir*, a biographical lexicon written by the Baghdadi historian Ibn Sa'd and published in eight volumes, the last of which is wholly devoted to the women of Medina.[4] The level of credibility of the Hadith concerning Umm Waraqa is considered authentic and reliable (Hadith literature, which stems from oral tradition, is classified into three categories: authentic, good and weak). Contrary to a widespread idea according to which early Muslim women were passive and confined to the home, several of them played active roles in the religion as teachers, warriors or even imams. The women imams were not very numerous; we know of three. In so far as the accounts of the Prophet's life only appeared in written form two centuries later, nothing forbids us from supposing that there weren't more women active in the nascent Islamic religion. At Mariam Mosque, we go back to the source of our religion, which is to know the Quran and the life of the Prophet Muhammad.

Among the first four caliphs who succeeded Muhammad after his death in 632, the first, Abu Bakr – who was the father of Aisha, the Prophet's third wife, and reigned for two years – approved of a female imamate as incarnated by his daughter. The opposite is true of the second caliph, Omar (634–644), known for his discrimination against women, who said they should be confined to the home. Today's conservative Muslims who defend patriarchy in Islam are disciples of this second caliph, who obviously could not claim any precedent set by the Prophet. When I lead Friday prayers in the company of the other women of Mariam Mosque, I often have Umm Waraqa, Umm Salama and Aisha in mind. Even if they've been dead for fourteen centuries, they are with me in my thoughts as if they were my contemporaries, my friends, my allies. I also think of contemporary Muslim feminists and other women leaders who, through their activism and writing, have allowed me to envisage this dream of female leadership in prayer. During the time of the Prophet, women already had various functions: some were teachers, warriors or imams. Furthermore, the Al-Azhar University in Cairo, as well as three of the four schools of Islamic jurisprudence, recognise that women have a basis for leading prayer for other women (only the Maliki school refuses). Ibn Rushd of Córdoba, better known under his Latinised name of Averroës (1126–1198), attested to the same thing in his encyclopedia of Islamic jurisprudence. Finally, al-Tabari (c. 839–923), a Muslim historian and scholar of the Quran, allowed women imams to lead prayer for both men and women. The same goes for distinguished Islamic scholars such as Abu Thawr (764–854), Ibn Arabi (1165–1240) and al-Muzani (791–878). But the majority of Muslim scholars of the past and of today do not allow women to lead prayer for a mixed-gender congregation.

Outside the study and exegesis of the sacred texts relating to the life and practices of the Prophet, our legitimacy as 'female imams' rests – and this is the second point – on the needs of believers and the demands of the 'community'. So, is there an expressed wish for female imams? If our Mariam Mosque remained empty of believers, then the answer would be clear. But women come to the mosque expressing their relief and happiness to find women imams who look like them and share their sensibilities. Some explain that they often feel isolated in their life as a believer, relegated to the back of the mosque, confined to a secondary category and separate rooms, not truly welcome. I myself have often felt this way:

in frustration, I've looked for a mosque that would be like a warm home, with a real sense of community and fellowship.

Those of our Christian friends who misunderstand Islam are stunned by the fact that Mariam Mosque appeared *sui generis*, without the authorisation of some religious authority, and enjoys total spiritual and legal independence. They forget that Islam, especially Sunni Islam, does not have clergy. Believers do not need an intermediary between themselves and God. The imam leads prayer, but does not in any way serve as a pivot between God and other believers. In the same way, in cases of sin, the believer repents by addressing the Creator directly, not by passing through another man or woman's mediation. As in Judaism, there is no clergy in the priestly sense. In Sunni Islam (and this is the main difference with Shi'a Islam), the imam is not a priest but a member of the community who leads prayer: he or she is 'the one who comes up front to lead the prayer'. There's no need to be a theologian; it's enough for an imam to be Muslim, wise, understand the pillars of Islam and know a large part of the Quran by heart to put themselves at the service of a religious congregation.

Islam is, therefore, for the most part, a 'decentralised' religion. While there is a Muslim hierarchy, it is not vertical. Muezzins perform the call to prayer. Imams lead the prayer and deliver the *khutbah*. Mosque directors run the mosque. Sheikhs must be of a mature age, scholars and chiefs of a clan or a Sufi order. Muftis are legal scholars: they can serve as arbitrators in cases of conflict on a particular subject and provide clarification on the interpretation of sharia law and the Hadiths. They can pronounce a fatwa – a legal statement on a specific matter. Qadis are judges in Islamic courts. Ulama (or mullahs, for Shi'ites) are scholars of Islam, guardians of the faith and traditions, and sources of reference. Sufi scholars devote themselves to the spiritual dimension of Islam; on the other hand, Shiism, which represents 10 to 15 per cent of the world's Muslims, mainly in Iran (80 per cent of the population), but also Iraq (over 50 per cent), Yemen (45 per cent), Lebanon (25 per cent) and Bahrain (over 50 per cent), recognises a clergy of several hierarchal levels, of which the highest is represented by the mullahs (under the titles of 'ayatollah' and 'Hujjat al-Islam').

Only women come to Mariam Mosque for the Friday prayer, but men are also welcome after 2 p.m. for Islamic spiritual care, marriages, conversions, the Aqiqah ceremony (for the birth of a child) and divorces. And that's without forgetting our 'Islamic academy', which offers teaching centred on Muslim history and culture, Islamic feminism, Arabic, philosophy and Sufism. This brings us to the third source of the legitimacy of a female imamate: experience and knowledge. Fundamentally, what is an imam? Muslims define the title in a variety of ways. Some define an imam as an Islamic scholar or spiritual leader of a community. For others, it is a person who leads prayer, works at a mosque, studies and teaches about the Quran, and accumulates knowledge. For me, an imam is a spiritual servant of the community; one who calls and leads prayers, delivers *khutbahs* (sermons), officiates at marriages, conversions and divorces, meets with believers for legal or spiritual counselling within the framework of 'Islamic spiritual care' and helps them resolve difficulties related to existential questions. An imam is not recognised by a degree or a nomination from higher powers, but by his or her own religious practice, knowledge, daily actions and exemplary behaviour, which imparts to him or her a spiritual form of existence in the universe. This path can be followed as much by a woman as it can be by a man.

However, before the opening of Mariam Mosque, many advise me to abandon the idea of adopting the title of imam. Some are detractors, of course, but others are friends, both male and female. 'Let it go, abandon the word "imam", call yourself something else – it's better for you to be associated with your academic titles rather than the religious title of imamah,' one of my closest friends suggests. From all sides, I'm told that adopting the title of 'spiritual guide' would be less controversial and more widely accepted, especially by traditionalist Muslims. Even my father is worried. After learning through a member of the family who lives abroad and the press that his daughter is going to become an imam, my father calls me to demand that I 'immediately' renounce this religious title. 'I thought you were going to direct this mosque from behind the scenes, not become one of its imams,' he says in a reproachful tone. I argue: 'Yes, that is the title I have chosen for myself, Baba. I believe words count. Claiming the title of "imam" has nothing trivial about it. It's fundamental. We're doing the same things as men. We're running a mosque, performing the call to prayer [*adhan*], delivering the *khutbah*, giving the *salat* [prayer] and the Friday prayer, giving legal and spiritual counselling, and offering Islamic spiritual care to Muslims who ask for our help. So, why shouldn't we adopt the title of imam?' It will take months for my father to come to grips with this new situation, but now he fully accepts it. And, once he discovered that there are many other mosques with female imams around the world, his worries subsided.

As for me, I like to underline the fact that I'm *in the process* of becoming an imam, *in the process* of learning how to lead a community and a mosque, *in the process* of tackling dilemmas and difficulties, and developing as an Islamic spiritual care person. I stay humble to the fact that I'm new to this area of running a mosque, and I'm continually looking for answers and seeking advice from Islamic scholars and those other women imams who came before me and who inspired me to walk on this path.

To tell the truth, the phenomenon of women imams is not new. In China, some women's mosques have existed since 1820. Female imams have been active since 1995 in South Africa, and since 2004–2005 in the United States and Canada, with a women's mosque opening in Los Angeles in 2015. In 2017,

Seyran Ateş opened a mosque in Berlin with mixed-gender prayer. But long before her, small groups of progressive Muslims in Germany have organised mixed-gender prayer services that are led alternately by men and women. Until very recently, the theologian and imam Halima Krausen, from the University of Hamburg, regularly delivered the *khutbah* during the Friday prayer service. 'Many Muslims, especially women, are angry', this translator of the Quran and a portion of the Hadiths explains in one of her works. 'They are angry about stereotypes from outside the Muslim community and ignorance and superstitions within Islam itself, where they are repeatedly challenged to react. This constant fight doesn't give them any time for constructive thought. They are angry because they feel cheated, betrayed, wronged of their spiritual and cultural inheritance. They are angry because they don't have time to work towards developing a modern interpretation of Islam and applying contemporary values in accordance with those they defend.'

Also in Germany, in the city of Cologne, another Muslim feminist, the theologian Rabeya Müller, has also been showing the way. In the 1990s, after converting to Islam, this pioneer cofounded the Zentrum für Islamische Frauenforschung und Frauenförderung (Centre for Islamic Women's Studies) and has developed a gender-neutral approach to reading the Quran in which women are equal to men: 'I see nothing in what is for me the relevant text, the Quran, that says that women shouldn't lead prayers. As long as the congregation that follows the prayers of the female preacher also supports her too, this is completely acceptable.'[5] In her view, women must make a personal effort to convince themselves that they are not men's assistants, but the co-authors of all aspects of Muslim life.

The inspiration for Muslims involved in the emancipation of women does not stem from the Western feminist movement of the 1960s and 1970s, but rather from around the world, especially in Muslim society. To simply call Mariam Mosque and Islamic feminism byproducts of the culture of the 1970s, with its 'flower power' and women's sexual liberation, would only feed the notion of Western superiority dominating over the East. Yet Egypt, among others, is one of the driving forces behind women's fight in the Middle East. For example, Nabawiyya Musa (1886–1951), who came from a middle-class family in Alexandria, became a pioneer of Egyptian and Arab feminism by being the first woman in her country to receive a high school education, in 1907. What's more, she did this as an external candidate since, at the time, women weren't allowed to attend universities under the laws imposed by Great Britain. From that point, she established herself as a public figure, publishing books and travelling around the Middle East giving talks on the rights of women and sexual violence. In 1923, she cofounded the Egyptian Feminist Union along with other remarkable women, including Huda Sha'rawi (1879–1947), who had already founded the Society for the New Woman. Based in a busy quarter of Cairo, this latter association enables impoverished girls to receive an education, offering them lessons in hygiene and other services.

The Egyptian Feminist Union aims higher: it defends the rights of women by demanding that they have access to college and public services. Huda Sha'rawi was involved in the nationalist fight to liberate her country from British rule. On returning from an international conference in Rome, she and Saiza Nabarawi decided to stop wearing the veil and lead their fight with uncovered faces, which earned them international renown. The Egyptian Feminist Union launched a bimonthly magazine in Arabic called *L'Égyptienne* in order to spread emancipatory ideas in the Arab world. Years later, this led to the organisation of the first Arab feminist congress in Cairo, which associated feminism with Arab nationalism. When the Arab League was created on 22 March 1945, Sha'rawi, ever the relentless activist, complained about the absence of women. 'The League whose pact you signed yesterday is only half of the League,' she argued, 'the League of half of the Arab people.'

The Egyptian feminist movement inspired a new generation of women activists in North Africa and the Middle East, including the Moroccan sociologist Fatima Mernissi (1940–2015), who was at the forefront of a new feminist paradigm in the 1980s, along with leading scholar Amina Wadud (the organiser of the mixed-gender prayer in New York in 2005) and other women intellectuals. Their idea – which is sadly not evident to all – was that women's roles evolve based on the transformation of familial and societal structures. They reread the Quran in the light of this reality and reinterpreted it in order to liberate women from the patriarchal structures and conservative traditions in Islam. In the United States, the historian Margot Badran (b. 1936), author of *Feminism in Islam: Secular and Religious Convergences*, theorises on and analyses feminism in Muslim societies and suggests that the notion of 'family' is a modern construct without basis in the sacred Islamic texts – which means that men and women are equal, since the Quran does not assign them specific roles. Badran therefore deeply calls into question the traditionalist idea that men and women are 'complementary', which lies at the core of what many Muslims believe.

'The religious principle of the full equality (*al-musawa*) of human beings (*insan*) is at the core of Islamic feminism', writes Badran. Gender equality is the basic principle; it is also the condition *sine qua non* of social justice, another priority of the movement. This equality must be played out in thought and action, and on the continuum that extends from the public sphere to the private sphere. 'A proclamation as clear as equality within the family and society in the religious framework of Islam constitutes a true historical breakthrough', Badran writes of the Muslim feminist movements. Like her and other Islamic feminist scholars, I am convinced that Muslim feminism is a force that will play a decisive role in surpassing male domination in Islam.

In Morocco, women who perform the same functions as we do are called morchidats ('guides' or 'religious teachers'). Their existence goes back to 2006 when the Moroccan state decided to establish a training programme for spiritual guides with the hope of preventing the spread of Islamic radicalism, after a series of five coordinated suicide attacks caused forty-one deaths in Casablanca three years earlier on 16 May 2003. Today, the Moroccan government finances the training of fifty spiritual guides every year, who work with women and young people in mosques, schools, villages, orphanages, hospitals, prisons or even villages in rural areas. In the Muslim world, such a positive initiative is unique, though morchidats are still not allowed to lead the Friday prayer, which remains the prerogative of male imams. Some people insisted I call myself a 'morchidat'; but at Mariam Mosque, women do lead the Friday prayer. And above all, how can we challenge the patriarchal structures in religions and claim to advocate for Islamic feminism if we don't dare to name things as they are?

This question is central. Often women are expected to interiorise their thoughts and soften their words in order to conform to masculine expectations. Be a good wife, a perfect mother, act wisely and in silence: this is what is sometimes –

often – demanded of women. They must declare themselves and claim the titles of 'imam' and 'rabbi' if they want to perform the same functions as their male counterparts.

I love walking along the water. In Copenhagen, I've certainly got it: the liquid element is everywhere. A walk through the capital, towards the Sound and across its canals, still preserves the ancient charm of port cities like this one. When I'm with my children, I love to visit the Little Mermaid, the statue inspired by Andersen's fairy tale, gracefully seated on a little rock outside the city. The route forces you to pass the Kastellet, the seventeenth-century citadel that served as the city's northern line of defence against its Swedish enemies. A little farther along is the Little Mermaid and, farther still, the industrial port where cruise liners moor their anchors. As a symbol of the city and one of its main tourist attractions, the statue is visited by thousands of tourists from all over the world. In general, they are surprised by her diminutive size: she is just over four feet tall. In the spring of 2016, among the crowd of anonymous visitors was the female rabbi Delphine Horvilleur. She and I had been invited to participate in a debate organised by the French Institute of Denmark and the Royal Library of Denmark on women's place in the 'religions of the Book'. Just before the debate, she made a courtesy call to the Mermaid. She later pulled a moral from the excursion for her speech, explaining to the audience that femininity today resembles the mermaid in the underwater world. 'If women want to exist in the open air, they, like the mermaid, must lose their voices. So they must face this alternative: be condemned to silence, or disappear back under the water. Neither the Quran nor the Talmud puts things quite this way, but it's the story we tell our children ... '

Delphine and I have a lot in common. We were born in the same year, we both have young children, we are both female religious leaders and face the same challenges. Our meeting was truly enjoyable. I was delighted to find a progressive Jewish woman whose spiritual approach compares with my own, with a profound sense of faith that goes beyond simply respecting rituals and traditions. During our public debate, we both recited passages from the sacred texts of our respective religions: she sang a song from the Jewish tradition, and I recited the first sura of the Quran. This shared moment was extended with a dinner, and we parted ways promising to meet again. Two years later, we would meet again in the Élysée Palace in France. We were both invited by Emmanuel Macron to give our reflections on faith and radicalisation and the role of Islam in Europe.

I love to remember, through the examples of the women activists and intellectuals both past and present mentioned above, that Mariam Mosque in Copenhagen is part of a long history. Our specific aim is to play our part and demonstrate that we are at the level of what can be called a feminist Islamic tradition. In this, we are aiming for excellence. While there is not currently a school for imams in Denmark, I believe that the Western university system is enough to build knowledge and establish our legitimacy. The first four imams or khatibahs who have served the Mariam Mosque during our first year all have higher intellectual training. Whether it comes to Islamic philosophy, the Arabic language or Islamic archeology, all of our women imams or khatibahs possess at the very least a master's degree, complemented in some cases by personal research projects and continual reading. I am moreover very happy to have received my education from a Western university, open minded and in touch with the world, along with my training in Arabic at Danish and Middle Eastern universities. It is important that all the women imams of Mariam Mosque have educations exempt from patriarchal values and doctrinal rigidity.

In any case, Mariam Mosque has created its own curriculum of Islamic studies, which will begin in 2018. It includes seventeen three-hour modules on Islamic philosophy, Islamic spiritual care, Sufism, cognitive therapy, Islamic feminism, *fiqh* (Islamic jurisprudence), the study of the Quran, leading the Friday prayer, the history of the Middle East, and other related topics over the course of a semester in order to train women believers to be imams and to train others, Muslims or otherwise, in these notions. This programme is open to candidates who already have solid credentials in the Arabic language, theology or a graduate degree related to Islam.

At the end of the programme, the candidates must be able to lead the Friday prayer and any other Islamic religious ceremony (*Aqiqah* birth ceremonies, marriages, conversions), have reached an acceptable level of *tajwid* (reciting the Quran), know how to practise *dhikr* (Sufi meditation), and can suitably represent the mosque and communicate with outsiders. Aspiring candidates are encouraged to obtain a master's degree in Islamic theology from the University of Copenhagen, subsidised by the mosque. Finally, the future women imams must have competencies in Islamic spiritual care and cognitive therapy. This is because one of the essential missions of an imam is to listen to believers' concerns and answer their questions regarding existential matters, psychological issues and even marriage difficulties. Knowing the Quran perfectly and being able to recite the suras is not enough. The imam must know how to act as a pastor, even a therapist, and be a good listener. An imam is not there to judge, but to listen. Islamic spiritual care is the opposite of offering advice. We don't tell people what they should do. We take care to guide them in a way that they can find their own solutions to their problems. Only in this way can an imam offer spiritual care to believers and help them find solutions, or at least comfort them. For my part, this dimension of being an imam is precisely my strong point, perhaps more than reciting verses.

Being an imamah is mostly about servanthood and every week people come for Islamic spiritual care. In the years preceding the opening of Mariam Mosque, I worked with girls and women subjected to mental abuse, through the Exit Circle, an NGO that I founded. As a result, our mosque is equipped to respond to the specific suffering faced by Muslim women who are exposed to physical or psychological abuse. Our fight for Islamic feminism is also in this sphere.

CHAPTER SEVEN

For my sisters

Man is born free, and everywhere he is in chains.

Jean-Jacques Rousseau (1712–1778)

On a weekly basis I, along with other personnel from Mariam Mosque, hold open consultation hours at the mosque offering Islamic spiritual care. In our office connected to the prayer hall, where I typically meet couples for preliminary interviews for marriage preparation, women and men come to me with questions about their married life, death, conversion, grief, their family and the myriad of life's difficulties. The room is spacious and furnished with a big white couch, a sizeable table, two chairs and a large antique handwoven carpet, with a revolutionary message covering most of the wall. These female visitors are looking for insights and advice, asking me to listen and, opening up to me like others might do with a pastor.

This is how, one day, a woman in her forties with North African roots comes to me. In her brown eyes, I can read infinite sorrow and loneliness. Suspecting the extent of her unhappiness, I invite her to sit down on the couch while I make her a cup of tea. I have the woman's permission to share her story here. She tells me that she lost a child, her daughter, who was ten years old. The woman's husband exposed her to emotional abuse, and regularly humiliated and hit her from the start of their marriage. And she felt terribly guilty. The reason? Her daughter, despite being gravely ill and very weak, tried several times to protect her from her husband's abuse. The sickly girl would put herself in her father's way when he became violent, but he would shout and push her away. But the child would return to the fray, hanging on to her father and trying in vain to hold him back. 'These images haunt me often,' the woman concludes. 'My daughter was defending me and I was incapable of protecting her. ... ' Over the course of the conversation, my visitor confesses to me that she feels responsible for her daughter's death. When she was pregnant, her husband punched her in the stomach, and she is convinced that the child's fragile physical state, then her death, were provoked by these violent episodes. 'I should've left, not put up with it, I was a coward ... '

As I'm addressing a believer, I apply the technique of 'Islamic spiritual care', one of the hallmarks of Mariam Mosque. This form of conversation is a mix of cognitive behavioural therapy and religious teaching based on the Quran and other Islamic texts.

I comfort the woman by telling her, for example, that in Islam, death is established by fate and is an inescapable fact. Such words might seem simplistic, yet they have the power to comfort those who are grieving. I talk about the Prophet Muhammad – blessed may he be – and his way of envisaging death and the beyond. However, even though faith is always of great assistance, explaining to someone in deep distress that 'things are written in advance' doesn't suffice. ... So, my expertise in cognitive behavioural therapy comes into play. For four years, I have been taking courses in cognitive therapy and, in the summer of 2018, after finishing my final year, I will receive a degree as a certified cognitive behavioural therapist.

Cognitive behavioural therapy is a concise, scientifically validated method that seeks to replace a person's negative ideas and ill-adapted behaviours with reactions consistent with reality. Based on an active relationship between the therapist and his or her patient in the learning of new behaviours, it allows the patient progressively to overcome debilitating symptoms such as stress, inhibitions, aggressive reactions or even mental distress stemming from physical suffering. For example, there is a way to ask questions that allows a person to replace automatic negative thoughts with other, more positive, ones. 'Did your husband hit you when you were pregnant with your other children? Did he hit you in front of them? Did he hit them?'

'Yes,' she answers.

'And are your other children still alive?'

'Yes, they are.'

I direct the conversation towards them in order to open up another field of thought. She then bursts into tears which, at this stage, is an encouraging, positive sign. After having held back her emotions and tears for so many years, now she 'decompensates' by crying for several minutes. For the first time, she is opening up her heart to someone whom she believes she can trust. It's a little as if she were meeting with a psychologist – but with one major difference: my interventions, as a form of spiritual care, are free. Moreover, our meetings include a religious dimension, because I integrate Quranic teaching wherever possible.

At Mariam Mosque, we seek to help women with all kinds of problems, including specific matters concerning divorce and violence, and both domestic and psychological abuse. Some of these women explain that when they meet with an imam to find comfort and advice, the best they can hope for (assuming they have even ventured to take such a step) is a terse response such as: 'Be patient' or even, 'Try to behave more like an exemplary spouse, and you'll see, everything will work out, insha'Allah!' My intentions are far from criticising my male colleagues. There are excellent mosques directed by remarkable imams who accomplish exemplary spiritual care – such as the Dansk Islamisk Centre (Danish Islamic Centre), which works in hospitals and prisons. However, there are also examples of male imams and mosque communities that neglect the needs of women subjected to violence and Muslim women's right to divorce in cases of severe violence. Some women find that certain male imams cannot really understand their specific needs and problems. Working in the field of psychological abuse, I've seen that in such situations it's not rare for women to meet with condescension, along with a patriarchal attitude marked with prejudice. The overwhelming majority of mosques do not grant women – including those who are abused – the right to initiate divorce proceedings. This is another thing that makes Mariam Mosque different, to which I'll return.

Our mosque, on the contrary, makes women its priority. This is our 'niche'. We worship God and we pray. But we are not content to simply recite the Quran. Because being an imam, male or female, means being available for others, listening to them, guiding them, offering them spiritual care. An imam is first and foremost a servant to the people, with the secondary responsibility of leading prayer. For my part, this dimension of servanthood takes up 80 per cent of my time. When Muslim women come knocking at our doors, they know they will find the assistance they are looking for. Our approach to Islamic spiritual care distinguishes us from other mosques.

In the skilled work of spiritual listening and guidance, I draw heavily from my experience in the Exit Circle, an NGO

I founded in 2014 that offers self-help groups to women (and girls) subjected to psychological abuse and social control. When I started working with the 'critical Muslims', I realised that the subject, especially psychological abuse, was coming up repeatedly in conversations with other women. Some had been victims. Others knew people who were living in such situations. As for me, in my own circle I've had the chance to watch the behaviour of certain abusive men who are capable of taking advantage of religious discourse in order to control or morally harass their wives or sisters. Beyond any religious context, this pretention to masculine supremacy draws on ancient roots: the hereditary conviction that men possess a natural right to exert domination over the female sex. Far from uniquely concerning Muslims, this attitude can be observed all the way up the social pyramid.

We all have our share of sorrow and happiness. I myself have been the victim of psychological abuse, not in my childhood or adolescence, but when entering adult life. I was subjected to religious social control and gradually went from being a strong and rebellious young woman to developing submissive tendencies in the way I acted and communicated with others. I was trying to cope with the situation and protect myself by pleasing the aggressor and keeping up appearances, but my cautious behaviour only kept the vicious circle going. I had a balanced childhood, loving parents, a solid network of close friends and a good education, but still I didn't feel like telling anyone about it. After all, I still saw myself as a strong woman, so this couldn't be happening to me. I was living in a sort of illusion of normality, yet I was distraught, unhappy and humiliated to find myself under the psychological control of another. Looking back, I realise now that most of the things I have since done in life, especially my activism, are rooted in my personal experiences with religious social control. And from that position, I made the real-life discovery that patriarchal structures do exist in our society. On an individual level, I could not find a way to free myself from my chains and get out of this situation. However, with the help of others, I managed to break free.

One of the worst consequences of psychological abuse is loneliness. When I felt alone and isolated, I looked for self-help groups for women subjected to psychological abuse. But I found none. Psychological violence was not even something that was officially recognised as a form of abuse back then. From there, the idea for the Exit Circle was born. At the time, I promised myself that I would one day set up an NGO that would come to the aid of the victims of psychological violence through the means of something like cognitive therapy groups. Several years later, in September 2014, I fulfilled this promise and founded the Exit Circle, whose slogan is simple: 'No to psychological violence and social control'. The name 'Exit Circle' references the circle (as in vicious circle, but also a meeting circle), while 'exit' stands for a way of getting out and finding a solution. The idea is to break the vicious cycle, to 'exit the circle'. Today, the organisation offers group therapy for up to ten girls or women. Seated in a circle, the participants meet for two hours once a week to anonymously share their life stories and experiences, with the hope of finding the strength to break the terrible cycle in which they are caught. By acquiring new cognitive abilities and sharing life experiences with others in identical situations, it becomes possible to break free from a harmful and persistent psychological hold.

Psychological abuse is a significant problem that happens in all social, religious and cultural environments. Yet its victims have no one to turn to and no place to go to other than shelters, which are often full and generally seen as a last resort. It is therefore necessary to treat the problem early so that victims have options other than what they see as their only choice. In Denmark, more than half a million people live alone in isolation or exclusion. The victims of psychological abuse are often part of this group. The work of the Exit Circle is preventative: the idea is to help victims before the problem escalates. By reducing the risk, we can preventatively reduce the cost of treatment, which can heavily affect public funds.

The Exit Circle, which runs therapy groups all over Denmark, is a secular, non-political organisation that aims to help all victims of psychological abuse, including social control and religious social control. Our mission is to extend and develop our programmes nationwide through a holistic approach based on three main concepts: breaking the law of silence, reinforcing the individual, and shattering hierarchies. First, by telling their individual stories, victims break the law of silence that surrounds psychological violence – a subject that is still taboo in our society. Honesty and openness to others allows us to dispense with taboos. Instead of each victim fighting silently in his or her own corner, they discover that members of a community can help each other by sharing their stories. Second, in the therapy groups, each victim is recognised and strengthened. Each person is no longer anonymous, but an individual in their own right, who shares their experiences, reaches out to others and therefore gives hope to those in the same situation. It is a virtuous circle. Finally, we seek to shatter hierarchies even within our own organisation. Our therapy groups rest on the idea that each person has something to contribute to the community, a part to play, allowing them to exit the connection between victim and aid.

The Exit Circle's self-help groups are unique to Denmark and the first of their kind. Our organisation differs from shelters and other social agencies because we offer weekly group therapy sessions. Above all, our universal approach to psychological violence and social control allows us to be deemed credible in all kinds of sociocultural environments.

While the Exit Circle focuses on preventative measures, it also offers personalised aftercare for those who are rebuilding their lives after leaving a psychologically abusive relationship or having recently finished one of our therapy cycles.

From the moment of its founding, the Exit Circle is an immediate success. After the first group begins in Amager, in the suburbs of Copenhagen, another opens in Nørrebro, a district within the capital, followed by a third in the port city of Aarhus a month later, and a fourth more recently in Odense, the birthplace of Hans Christian Andersen, in the southern part of the country. For the last few years, I have been working as a full-time volunteer, putting together and managing a team of forty other volunteers and staff members. In 2017, I was finally able to obtain city grants and private funds that will allow us to extend our reach and open up our groups to boys and men subjected to psychological violence as well. The Exit Circle fulfils a much-needed social mission. Led by a tight-knit team of six key workers (three of whom are paid staff members), the organisation relies on the expertise of psychologists, a sexologist, a sociologist of religion and several psychology students, social workers, jurists, cognitive behavioural therapists and senior business developers, along with several experienced women and men who were former victims of psychological abuse or social control.

The Exit Circle is committed to fighting received ideas about psychological abuse such as: it only affects weak women;

it is less serious than physical abuse; or it mainly concerns populations of Muslim origin or third-world countries. Let me be clear: today, the majority of women (seven in ten) treated by our network are non-Muslim Danes. Domestic abuse, whether in the couple or the family, is the illness of our times, and it is invisible, silent and widespread. It is not connected to a specific religion and affects every culture. It's an invisible plague in our daily lives, which from the outside often appear deceptively perfect. As shown in *Hamlet*, Shakespeare's masterful work, we must never forget that the world is a theatre of illusions. Nothing is as it seems.

Some of the women from the Exit Circle have shared their stories publicly in order to break the taboo surrounding psychological abuse to women, in the hope of motivating other women to do the same and ultimately to break the silence around the topic. One of these brave women, whom I will call Sara, is a Dane and a Muslim convert. She was the first woman to seek help from the Exit Circle in 2014, which at the time had only five volunteers. I remember all the women who have come to us, but Sara left a particular impression on me. A fragile Danish woman in her forties, she married a North African man, converted to Islam not long after they met, and has since had six children with him. 'Little by little,' Sara told me, 'he started to control my thoughts, my social calendar, my life. He forbade me from seeing my family and girlfriends, from taking our children to the playground, from studying, watching TV or even having a mobile phone.' She quickly found herself isolated, without a social life, cut off from the world, under the psychological control of her children's father. 'He would bring me books from the library, and that was how I educated myself. I asked all the imams I met in the local mosque to help me with my abusive husband, but they all just told me to try harder and to be patient. One day, a local imam came to our house with his wife. I confided in her about the abuse, isolation and mental terror I was being subjected to. She told me to pack my things, take the children and go find help. My encounter with this woman, who actually took my words seriously, was a turning point for me. I fled the house with five of my children. I couldn't bring the oldest, since he was sixteen and had already been damaged by his father's manipulative and violent behaviour.' After sixteen years of marriage, Sara managed to escape and find refuge in a centre for abused women. It's there that she heard about the Exit Circle.

She had made it to 'the other side', but she still needed to build a new life for herself and her children. This meant learning to reintegrate into society, rebuild her self-esteem and repair all the broken relationships with her family and friends. In the Exit Circle, taking inspiration from cognitive behavioural therapy, we help women identify and challenge their negative thoughts and unhelpful behaviours in order to get out of the 'safe zone' into which they've withdrawn. Sara had been isolated from society for sixteen long years. As a result, she was afraid of going out in public. I took her to a nearby café and we had a cup of tea, sitting among strangers. This took a considerable effort on Sara's part. Gradually, she returned to real life. Slowly, thanks to her willingness, along with the Exit Circle's therapy groups and psychological aftercare, she managed to rebuild herself. Today, she has regained her freedom and independence, but her ex-husband kept parental custody of four of their six children.

This story sums up social control within a marriage. It's an invisible form of suffering that doesn't leave bruises, even though it destroys the soul. Do you feel like you're walking on eggshells? Do you feel like you're being watched, manipulated, mocked, patronised, ridiculed or threatened? Have your boundaries been crossed? Have you been yelled at, cursed at, humiliated, isolated, followed in public, spied on, interrogated, ignored or criticised? When these circumstances become your everyday life, you are a victim of mistreatment and psychological abuse.

Psychological abuse is the influence of a manipulative person who criticises you, controls your thoughts, your actions, what you read, your diversions, your dreams; who decides your hobbies, your purchases, whom you see and when, what you wear. It's a prison with transparent bars. Someone is always at your side, enforcing their rules at every moment, without warning, maybe even with a smile. They demotivate you, isolate you, threaten to kill you if you ever leave them, tell you you're a bad mother, wife, girlfriend, daughter, that you're useless, ugly, worthless. They ignore you, then a second later they love you, but then they push you, reject you, deny you again. Psychological violence takes a variety of forms and often has a repetitive, systematic dimension. It sometimes surpasses language and words. It can be a feeling, looks, sighs. Your cooking is bad. You make too much noise when you drink a glass of water. You don't take care of your family, your children. Your laugh is annoying. Your voice is too low or too high, your skin too pale or too dark.

One woman confessed to me that she always had to ask her husband's permission to go shopping for groceries, and afterwards he had to see the receipt. He would regularly consult the history on her mobile phone to see to whom she had spoken and for how long. In sum, it's a neurotic form of harassment that can take diverse forms such as stalking, when obsessive attention is paid to a woman in order to intimidate or scare her, and includes following or watching her. Psychological violence can be economic: the victim is dispossessed of her financial autonomy and her resources are controlled by her husband; or material: he destroys her things, a book, a mobile phone, a computer or something valuable to her; or sexual: when the husband imposes sexual relations on his wife without her consent, he is raping her or threatening to rape her. Some married women have sex on a weekly basis against their will.

At the level of physical abuse, mental abuse is included. But this is problematic, because unlike physical assault, psychological violence is impossible to prove and doesn't leave traces. What's more, it isn't illegal in many countries, including Denmark, even though the Danish government signed the Istanbul Convention that criminalises psychological abuse. Psychological abuse is therefore the ideal weapon for manipulation – and with dangerous consequences: isolation, loneliness, shame, guilt, stress, depression, anxiety, and for young people, dropping out of school or college. It's best if the violence can be counteracted before the victim has entirely submitted to their torturer, as Sara did for over a decade, and has been destroyed as a result. Fortunately, this is possible. Even in cases where victims are sunk in deep depression, there is always hope. When suffering becomes insupportable and a victim opens up to a psychologist or therapist, or by joining the Exit Circle, then a way out is feasible.

To get out of the trap, victims of psychological abuse have just three options: flight, fight or submit. In the beginning stages of psychological violence, most people fight back. But unfortunately in the later stages, the majority of people, both children and adults, often end up choosing the third option. By instinct, they devote all their efforts to calming the situation by developing submissive communication with the aggressor. This automatic, unconscious submission mechanism aims at self-protection called 'security behaviour'.

By accepting a form of submissive communication, the victim seeks to normalise an abnormal situation. We see this type of reaction with abused women as well as children in abusive situations.

Claiming that the practice of social control in the family can be explained entirely by the archaism of a certain religion or cultural determinism is a profound error. Religion often has very little to do with it, even though in some cases it is manipulated by aggressors, who use it to justify their harm. The group therapy sessions in the Exit Circle, as well as the spiritual care offered at Mariam Mosque, seek to help victims of violence affirm themselves with words, take back power, and distance themselves from a position of submission. A young Muslim woman, aged twenty-six, explained to me during her time with the Exit Circle that she had submitted to her mother's control. The mother had forbidden her daughter from seeing her friends, but allowed her to have a job. In order to escape her mother's control, the daughter had to lie and say she had two jobs. The mother also forced her to ask permission for everything but would always refuse to grant it. This young woman's attitude was natural, since she was under a considerable amount of psychological pressure: the one who must submit disregards their own self and thinks only about how to satisfy the needs of the person in control. The first step the young woman and I took together was allowing her to identify her own 'security behaviour'. Employing techniques from cognitive behavioural therapy, I asked her what she thought would happen if she simply *told* her mother her plans rather than asked for her permission. Even the idea of this suggestion terrified her. So her first behavioural experiment was to tell her mother, in a detailed manner, that her friend Freja would be picking her up on a Monday at 5 p.m. and take her to go see a film, then they would have dinner together and return home at 9 p.m. at the latest. And it worked. The mother said yes because, for the first time, her daughter had simply told her mother what she was doing rather than asked for permission. Monday is also a quieter day compared to Friday or Saturday, when people are out drinking and partying. This brief example shows that cognitive behavioural therapy, through the slightest actions or words that may appear insignificant, can allow a person to change the way they see things and, sometimes, to alter the course of their life.

The Exit Circle, as I've already said, is a secular, non-political NGO. It is not reserved exclusively for women, even though they make up the majority of those we see. One of our most emblematic volunteers is a man who, before working for us, was the victim of psychological abuse. The plague of abuse is universal and exists in every area of society. Another form of manipulation that is just as problematic is 'religious social control'. This is when religion is used as a weapon to dominate another person such as a child, wife or husband. The perpetrator can be a man or parent seeking to control how the woman or children in the family dress, such as forcing them to wear the hijab or the burqa, or forbidding them from seeing *kuffar*. Sometimes, this form of social and religious control goes to the point of forcing a woman to marry a Muslim man, sometimes even from a specific country.

I am the founder and leader of both Mariam Mosque and the Exit Circle. While the two are of different natures – one is secular, the other religious – both seek to challenge patriarchal structures and suppressive mechanisms by working to strengthen women's rights, whether in the family, society or religious institutions. Before Mariam Mosque opened, I held my first Islamic spiritual care consultation in my own home office. A woman of Iraqi origin, whom I will call Safia, came with her mother to seek an Islamic divorce. As soon as she sat down in front of me, I could tell she was a brave woman. Her problem, a major one, was that she was married to a man who was beating her and her children. One of the children, a boy, was beaten on a weekly basis for a number of years. Safia moved far away from her husband and he was convicted in court. She explained to me that she had just obtained permission for the divorce in a civil court, but it was not enough. As a Muslim believer, she also wanted to validate this decision before God. She contacted dozens of imams in Denmark, but none of them agreed to give her an Islamic divorce, called a *khula*. I stood next to her while she called another imam, only to witness him refuse her as well. Determined to prevent the separation, her husband had categorically refused to agree to a divorce according to Islamic law.

However, some of the imams had nevertheless advised Safia to contact an Islamic court in London. The British capital actually houses several of these official institutions (there are over thirty across the United Kingdom) that, with the implicit agreement of the state, are authorised to implement the law according to sharia principles. These 'sharia courts' mainly deal with marriages and divorces,but they can be bureaucratic and expensive, which she wanted to avoid. I decided to start divorce proceedings under the aegis of Mariam Mosque. Beforehand, I took care to contact some imams in Denmark to try to have them reason with the violent husband and attempt reconciliation once more, because Islam advises amicable separation. But, out of fear of exposing themselves to threats or a violent reaction, they refrained from following up with him and asking for the divorce Safia was entitled to.

First, I started to evaluate the risks of such a procedure … before finally concluding that we shouldn't live in fear. If someone comes to me asking for help, how can I close the door on them? That would be contrary to Allah's teaching and my own convictions. Yet as I've already said, an imam's main mission is to serve their community of believers. This can involve risks, and it's not rare for imams to receive threats from violent husbands. But many of the choices we make in life are risks. As for me, I'd rather see things in a positive light. Because I'm convinced that every time you open a door by doing a good thing, God recognises it and opens the doors of His house even wider, in order to help you help others.

A few weeks after my first meeting with Safia, she returned to Mariam Mosque – which had opened in the meantime – and came to our Friday prayer service with her civil divorce certificate and other civil documents in hand. Having pulled together enough witness statements and documents (including a conviction for violence against her son), Mariam Mosque started drawing up the *khula*, the certificate for the termination of an Islamic marriage, based on reasoning from Islamic sacred texts concerning cases of violence. At the same time, we contacted one of the sharia councils in London through a spiritual brother from our supportive committee group who lives there. On our side of the process, we produced this text: 'We, Mariam Mosque, declare with the present act the termination of the Islamic marriage between Safia and her husband Hassan. The reasons for termination are as follows. The Danish court recognises that Hassan has engaged in repeated acts of violence against his son; Hassan has engaged in acts of violence on a daily basis against his wife Safia; Hassan has been condemned by a Danish court by reason of his acts of violence against the couple's only child and is at present not authorised to see them. The Quran forbids violence and the Prophet Muhammad, may peace be with him, says the following on the subject: "A perfect Muslim is he from whose hand and tongue mankind is safe. / The best among you is he who is good to his wife. / He who is bad to children is not one of us. / Power consists of being able to control oneself when anger arises. God is gentle and loves gentleness."

'In addition, this is what the Quranic texts say on the subject of the husband's consent: "The majority of schools agree that the husband's consent is essential for obtaining a divorce. However, other interpretations suggest that the husband's consent is not necessary in case of certain circumstances, such as cruelty (*darar*). In almost all cases, a woman can produce conclusive evidence to obtain divorce." This is the case with Safia. On account of the violence inflicted by her spouse and the danger incurred, reconciliation is not possible. According to the law of termination of an Islamic marriage, the termination of this marriage can be pronounced for the following reasons: the husband has disappeared for four years; the husband has neglected to provide for household needs; the husband has been condemned to seven years of prison or more; the husband has not fulfilled his marital duty for at least three years; the husband's behaviour has been deranged for at least two years; the wife was a minor at the time of marriage; the husband treats his wife with various forms of cruelty (including physical abuse, verbal aggression, moral harassment, sexual abuse and threats); the husband has disposed of his wife's property; the husband is obstructing his wife's' religious practice. Copenhagen, 14 October 2016.' Several months after Mariam Mosque issued the Islamic divorce to Safia, the sharia council in London issued a divorce to her as well, on behalf of the evidence we put forward to them.

So, besides specialising in Islamic spiritual care, Mariam Mosque is one of the rare places, along with the Danish Islamic Centre, that gives women the right to divorce. In the United Kingdom, some women are also working hard to resolve the difficulties Muslim women face in obtaining a divorce. There are now certain places in the country where Muslim women can secure their divorce, including one sharia council presided over by a female qadi (judge). She and many others are helping Muslim women procure a divorce in the United Kingdom. But despite all these efforts to defend women's rights, the problem of women being allowed to obtain a divorce remains worldwide.

In many countries in Europe and the Muslim world, women's right to divorce is not included in marriage contracts, even though it is lawful under Islamic law. Our marriage contracts take this scenario into account. That's why women today trust us, consult with us and dare to open up to us when their husbands turn to domestic abuse. At Mariam Mosque, they can get a divorce (naturally after having explored all possibilities for reconciliation) and this is starting to be recognised … all the way to the United Kingdom. In fact, I receive a call one day from the House of Commons in the UK Parliament, who wish to consult me about the *khula*, or the divorce proceedings initiated by a woman. We chat over Skype and set up a video conference for a later date, which I imagine will be one to one. On the appointed day, I get home late and out of breath because I've rushed to pick up the children from school. Some of the staff at Mariam Mosque are waiting for me in the living room to start the videoconference. We open my MacBook Pro and, once the connection is established, I discover that the meeting isn't an intimate conversation with a Parliament representative, but with all the Members of Parliament seated in the House of Commons, where my face is projected on to a giant screen.

Since I haven't even had time to take off my coat or catch my breath, I ask them for five more minutes. … Then, after giving a presentation about Mariam Mosque, a discussion begins. In the United Kingdom, some imams refuse to implement divorces initiated by women. I explain my philosophy: 'It's useless and counterproductive to demonise imams from the outside; it's better to change things from within, through actions.' On my screen, one female MP remarks: 'Since we don't have a mosque for women in our country, we have no other choice but to sanction wayward imams … ' Her words resonate with me: 'We don't have a mosque for women …

' and in my head, I finish her sentence: 'but it will happen.' I'm convinced that Mariam Mosque is only the outpost of a movement that, in the twenty-first century, will win more battles for women's rights both within and outside Islam.

CHAPTER EIGHT

Through earth, fire, air and water

Let's be careful with each other
so we can be dangerous together.

Unknown

On my thirty-fifth birthday, my two close friends and neighbours, Lena and Naraya, who are like sisters to me and whose children are my children's best friends, give me an unforgettable gift they call 'the journey of the soul': a kind of quest for the self. One Saturday at noon, they show up at my house and hand me a small red suitcase. I open it with excitement and – surprise! – inside I find a four-page letter requiring me to become more familiar with the four elements – earth, fire, air and water – by confronting them both outside and inside myself. My friends ask me to choose three things that I want to bring into my life and three things I want to abandon; then, to find objects symbolising these things and put them in the red suitcase to bring on the 'journey'. Since they believe I have already mastered air, because I'm creative, fast-thinking, a visionary, etc., they want me to explore the other elements: earth, fire and water.

My first challenge consists of going into the forest at night. I must stay there alone for a while, in order to face my fear in the total darkness. My mischievous friends know what I'm afraid of: solitude isn't my thing. And much less in a Scandinavian forest in the middle of autumn. ... The idea, they insist with all seriousness, is to confront my fear, listen to it and discover what the fear of being alone signifies and tells me about myself. Why am I afraid of the dark? How can I conquer the fear of being alone in the darkness? After sunset, they blindfold me and lead me deep into the woods. Once we arrive, they uncover my eyes, confiscate my mobile phone and tell me they'll be close by, then disappear. ... I discover that sixty minutes can feel like an eternity. I've rarely felt so attentive to nature, keeping my ears open to the sound of the wind, the scratching of branches, the noises of animals and insects. Afterwards, I felt so happy, having confronted and overcome my fear. ...

The second challenge bears the signature of my friend Naraya, who has mastered fire to perfection, thanks to her past as a fire dancer performing at sacred temples in India and medieval markets in Denmark. She shows me how to make a bonfire and light torches. Then she teaches me how to dance while twirling long poles lit at the ends. It's a very precise and ancient art. This fire challenge, my friend explains, represents the challenges of life and how to hold on when everything around you is falling apart or bursting into flame.

Next, my friends take me to the Sound, still with the red suitcase, and invite me to swim in the cold water and throw the three objects symbolising what I want to get rid of in my life into the water. In the little red suitcase, I have brought a mirror, representing vanity; a photo of myself, representing my ego and great ambitions; and an extract from 'One Art', a poem by Elizabeth Bishop, which illustrates illusions and the art of losing or letting go. This third and last challenge is the most enjoyable: swimming in the sea that separates Sweden and Denmark. Despite the cold – in the autumn, the water temperature doesn't even reach ten degrees centigrade – I enjoy it. In fact, even though my zodiac sign is Libra, an air sign, water has always been my element. From childhood, I've felt the need to be in contact with the liquid element on a daily basis. I love swimming, and the rain even more. As a child, when I was sad, it only took doing a few breaststrokes to transform my melancholy into positive energy. My mother often took me and my sister swimming in the sea, which was right by my childhood home. Today, I continue this tradition and regularly take my four children to the sea after dinnertime, to the great astonishment of the other mums in the neighbourhood. They assume that at such a late hour (8 p.m.), small children are better off in their pyjamas and in bed.

I swim almost every day, as the Sound is only three minutes away from our house by car. Owing to my occupation as an imam, I must be vigilant, aware of needing to present myself in a way that won't invite controversy. So, when I take my children swimming in public places, I wear a burkini that I made myself.

The deplorable 'burkini controversy' that made headline news across France (and the world) in the summer of 2016 affected me greatly. A woman was photographed on a beach on France's Côte d'Azur wearing the Muslim swimsuit. The picture made the news and spread all over the internet. French mayors in the area immediately wanted to ban the clothing item that, in their opinion, upset public order. It was an entirely erroneous argument and was quickly refuted by the French courts, invalidating the anti-burkini municipal decrees made along the Riviera. The public officials clearly confused the burkini and the burqa. In fact, outside the similar-sounding names, the two items of clothing have nothing in common.

Far from symbolising confinement or submission to Muslim fundamentalism, the burkini is a practical, modest outfit that allows Muslim women to enjoy swimming in the sea. For some women, it's even a sign of emancipation. In fact, the Quran says nothing about how women should dress when they go swimming. Muslim women who have started going to the beach over the last few decades used to have to stay on the sand and keep their veils on. When a woman wanted to go swimming, she only had two choices: take off her clothing, put on a swimsuit and feel almost naked, or go into the water fully clothed, which is hardly practical, especially as the fabric sticks to the skin when coming out of the water.

The burkini offers a third option for women who, in so far as they are taking the initiative to go to the beach, are freeing themselves from the dictates of rigid, conservative Muslims who claim that women don't need to go to the seaside and go swimming with men. By far, certain Islamists are the ones who want to ban the burkini. In sum, with all due respect to those mayors along the Côte d'Azur, the burkini isn't a propaganda tool meant to promote Islam. However, in the media storm surrounding the affair, fed by social networks on the lookout for the latest buzz, the 'controversy' gave the permission to make Muslims the scapegoat – and to caricature both the burkini and Islam, without any explanation.

This debate over the burkini is, in fact, linked to a broader one over the place of Islam in secular societies. Discussions concerning Muslims in European countries often turn around the question of 'loyalty' (concerning the country of residence) and whether European Muslims are truly able to embrace secularism; as if secularism is the only thing that can guarantee human rights, democracy and equality. ... Loyalty is often confused with a specific definition of secularism:

non-religiosity. As a result, religiosity is often seen as something opposed to modernity, and therefore potentially dangerous.

Secularism is not necessarily a guarantee of democracy. Still, I believe that some forms of secularism are an effective way to promote democracy and view all religions as equal. Secularism derives from the Latin word *saeculum*, which means profane and historically limited in time, as opposed to the sacred eternity beyond time. At its roots, secularism was opposed to any kind of religious dogma and rigid thinking, but not against religion in general. Since the 1920s, secularism has often been used as a form of liberation from religious authorities and norms, but it is not identical with non-religiosity. It is opposed to dogmatic thinking or practice, not religion.

Defining secularism is not easy, and academics, politicians and the media have proposed a variety of definitions. Secularism does not confine itself to a singular norm, and so it is more fitting to speak of secularism as a pluralistic term that people perceive in different ways. For some, secularism is a clear separation between religion and politics, as in France and Canada, countries founded on the model of a secular state. But another way to view secularism is as a dialogue between religion and politics, with a recognition and appreciation of religious values as an asset to society. Religion must not claim superiority; rather, it ought to accept a universal discourse, one in which religious arguments are represented and accepted alongside non-religious ones. Mariam Mosque represents this position. For us, viewing secular discourse as rational, and religious discourse as irrational is problematic. The state must be neutral, not favouring either secularism or religious ideas. It is there to maintain an equal balance between the two.

Secularism is carried out and defined in very different ways. It is possible to combine Islam and secularism, to practise one's faith in a secular society and to be a secular Muslim, if one defines secularism as a dialogue between religion and politics. A secular state can perfectly guarantee the same rights to all religions. However, the state must acknowledge the spiritual and religious dimensions of all religions and give them room for religious practice in society. The real question is not whether Muslims choose to associate religion and politics, but how. Within this sphere, the question of women's rights is essential.

It is a mistake to think that the way forward is to ask Muslims to denounce the belief that the Quran is the word of God in order to test whether they are 'devoted members of democracy'. Perhaps it would be more constructive to consider what secularism can and should entail, as a means to determine how exclusive or inclusive it should be. It is a conversation and a dialogue that should include and be beneficial to us all, in particular Islamist communities that tend to reject the notion of secularism even in Western societies. In doing so, they join far-right political parties across Europe by tightening the Gordian knot between Islam and the West.

Let's go back to the burkini, and even before. Like the burkini, the headscarf was also the object of misunderstanding, misinterpretation and distortion. Here also it's important to distinguish between the hijab, the burqa, the niqab and the chador. The wearing of the veil has been attested since antiquity in the Bible; it thus precedes the advent of Islam. The hijab, which comes from an Arabic word meaning 'to hide', 'to remove the gaze' or 'to distance', is a headscarf that covers the hair, the ears and the neck. Some politicians want to ban it. The burqa is the traditional dress worn mainly in Afghanistan. In the West, it has become the symbol of the Taliban regime. It is a long veil, often blue or brown, that covers the entire body and head, with a cloth grille that hides the eyes. The niqab is the full veil worn in many Arab countries. It is completed by a piece of fabric that completely covers the face with a split opening for the eyes. Promoted by Wahhabite Islam, the niqab has spread to urban locales in recent years, even though certain countries, such as France, have banned it (the burqa is also banned, while the chador and the hijab are banned only in educational establishments). Some women wear the niqab with sunglasses and gloves so that they can be covered entirely. Finally, the chador is a traditional Iranian headscarf, worn mainly by Muslim women in both urban and rural areas of Iran and some countries in central Asia.

These various veils are worn according to local traditions and individual interpretations. In Western countries, wearing the veil most often signifies a choice taken by women who want to affirm their Muslim identity or who see it a spiritual act. However, some men – as I said in the previous chapter – take advantage of sartorial traditions to impose their laws on women and force them to submit. They twist religion for political or personal ends. As for me, I rarely wear a veil, other than when I'm praying or performing Islamic rituals. And for that, I'm either at Mariam Mosque or at home, where I unroll my mat as soon as my iPhone app calls me to pray by letting off a prerecorded chant from a muezzin. On Fridays, at the mosque, some of the women pray 'uncovered', or without a veil, and we don't take any offence – because you can't measure someone's faith by a piece of cloth. I believe it's every woman's right to decide whether to wear a headscarf or not. It's her choice. Muslim women have different interpretations of what it means to be a modest woman. In the Universal Declaration of Human Rights, it is stated very clearly that everyone has the right to practise his or her religion in both public and private. Even though all the European countries signed the declaration, the headscarf is still debated and demonised throughout Europe, where the concept of neutrality often overshadows the concept of freedom of religion. However, if a woman or a girl is forced to wear a headscarf or anything else, it is a violation of her rights, which we must fight against.

In the West, the conception of the relationship between Islam and sexuality is often too simplistic. The 'Arab woman' or 'Muslim woman' is sometimes described as a stiff, fully covered, a sexual being or a mystically erotic individual. Such representations mainly stem from the view of the Middle East and Islam made popular by Orientalism, the nineteenth-century artistic and literary movement in the West. Contrary to these ideas, the Islamic religion is not afraid of the body or even of sexuality. Within the Sufi tradition, the love of God is often expressed through feminine metaphors and an earthly, romantic love. In such a depiction, the longing for the beloved often signifies the longing for the eternal divine God. Sometimes, Sufi poets even describe the love of God metaphorically as one man's longing for another young man – instead of a woman – thereby transcending or challenging traditional views of gender and sexuality.

Some passages of the Quran evoke sexuality in love because it favours harmony between a husband and wife, along with tenderness and affection. According to the Prophet, everything connected with earthly love is blessed. 'I loved your world: women, perfume and prayer', he said, illustrating the humanistic character of early Islam. Across the centuries, Persian and Arab intellectuals and poets have directly evoked the theme of sexuality and love, such as in the legendary seventh-century poem 'Layla and Majnun' by Qays Ibn al-Mulawwah, which tells of Majnun's tragic and indefatigable quest for his beloved Layla. Romantic love occupies a primary place in the Arab-Islamic world: there are no less than thirty words in Arabic for love. According to the Prophet, sexuality is an act of faith and a right within marriage. 'Getting married is accomplishing half of religion', the Quran says. The life of the couple occupies an essential place in Islam. And that's not all: contrary to received ideas (such as the way contemporary Muslims are characterised as puritanical and repressive in regard to sexuality), Islam does not forbid human beings from pleasure; on the contrary, it encourages believers to provide them with it.

In any case, sexual relations must remain acts derived from romantic feelings. The Quranic text insists on this aspect of married life. In Arabic, the word *nikah* means both marriage and penetration. As a believer and a romantic, I like the idea that every sexual act must take place within the context of marriage. In remaining faithful to one's spouse, you can better protect your heart, which houses the soul, as well as the hearts of others. But at the same time I think it's wise to get to know one's partner before marrying and I recommend that young people get to know each other well before marriage. Having a boyfriend or a girlfriend before marriage is wise and compatible with the Islamic concept of modesty, I believe. This is what I will explain to my four children: abstinence protects hearts but knowing your partner well before marriage is also important. A good friendship serves as a wise fundament for a marriage. They can do what they wish with this advice, but I won't impose rules on them without providing an explanation. Too many parents make this mistake: the rule then becomes a dogma deprived of meaning ... and efficacy.

One thing is certain: contemporary times put our hearts, our souls and our romantic feelings through a harsh ordeal. Many of our contemporaries are losing sight of the magic of seduction that is authentic eroticism, which clearly has nothing in common with the degrading images that can be found all over the internet. We can learn to protect our hearts; this comes with respecting our bodies. And respecting others. The Quran recommends not committing adultery in order not to interfere with the relationship existing between two beings united both romantically and spiritually.

Sometimes young couples come to the mosque asking me for marital counselling before they get married. I explain to them that they have to find their own balance. Love, seduction and eroticism can be based on distance and modesty but most importantly love is based on friendship and spiritual intimacy. When choosing a life partner you have to find one you can talk to, a spiritual soul mate, because one day you might find yourself in a situation where all you can do is talk. In Arab societies, there is a distance that men must keep publicly in relation to women, in order not to offend them. The Arab collective unconscious is characterised by modesty, the distance between men and women. This model is not necessarily to be taken literally. But in the game of seduction, the notion of distance is an important parameter that nourishes desire and a certain type of eroticism.

Islam does not require imams – or believers – to be without sin. Yet too often, Muslims enter a mosque with this binary view: they think they have to be perfect to be welcomed into the house of God. Some Muslims see the world in black and white, influenced by an oppressive, dogmatic view of religion. They are obsessed with the idea of perfection and want to appear as perfect, exemplary believers. But this goal is impossible to attain. Indeed, only Allah is exemplary and perfect; on the other hand, imams, like believers, are only imperfect humans. The goal of perfection is unattainable by its very nature. I consider faith to be like a path towards God. In following it, believers make mistakes. It's these mistakes that allow us to grow as people. To me being an imam is also about daring to show my own vulnerability and fallibility. By doing so I connect at a deeper level with the youth because they can mirror themselves in me. Nobody dares or wants to speak to a person who is perfect.

The other day, a young man came to ask me if it would be wise to get married to a woman he hadn't known for very long. I told him he was free to make his own choice, but in my opinion, it was worth getting to know each other before making such a commitment. But sometimes the intuitions of love are stronger than my advice, and quick marriages can turn out to be as solid as any other. In every case, it's important to be flexible, rather than rigid, in one's interpretation of divine guidance.

As an imamah, I'm contacted on a weekly basis by young people who want to know whether God allows them to marry a person from another religion. Some are embarrassed about the strict education of their parents, which does not accept interfaith marriages. This issue is one of the biggest dilemmas of our time. The fact is that Muslims living in the West have a high possibility of falling in love with a non-Muslim. That is why, as imams, scholars and intellectuals, we must seek to find Islamic solutions to such existing quandaries. Since I myself am the product of an interfaith marriage (Muslim father, Christian mother), I feel that I have a strong background from which to offer advice on such matters. My own experience as a child of such a union was positive, since my parents deeply respected each other without any intention of changing the other. If the parents of a couple entering into an interfaith marriage can manage to find harmony between the two cultures and religions, then the outcome will be a happy one and the children will be doubly reinforced by the priceless riches of a dual culture.

Since the founding of Mariam Mosque, I have officiated over more than twenty-six marriages, half of them interfaith ones between Muslim women and Christian men. It's often claimed that the Quran forbids interfaith marriages, but if you ask me, this is a myth and a question of interpretation. In fact, it is stated clearly that Christians and Jews belong to 'the People of the Book' and that they worship the same God as Muslims. Sura 5:5 says that Muslim men can marry People of the Book; but on the other hand, can Muslim women marry Christians or Jews? The Quran does not specify either way. However, in Sura 2:221, God says that both men and women should seek partners who are devoted to the One God. We must remember that the Quran is open to interpretation. If we accept the notion that Muslim men can marry Jewish or Christian women, then we must recognise the latter as believers who worship the One God. From this, we see that the Quran defends gender equality, including in interfaith marriages. Nevertheless, marrying polytheists is forbidden, because they were at war with Muslims at the time the Quran was revealed.

There is an overall consensus among Muslim scholars, fuqaha (jurists) and ulama (theologians) that an interfaith marriage between a Muslim woman and a non-Muslim man is forbidden, even if he is a Jew or a Christian. In my opinion, this prohibition is based on general opinion between mere mortals and masculine preconceptions (according to which women are fragile beings) rather than on Quranic principles. Many fear that if a Muslim woman marries a Christian man, their children will automatically become Christians. However, a growing number of Muslim scholars and activists disagree with this view, and have made their opinion known in their writing or activism. The Moroccan feminist and author Asma Lamrabet is one such activist. In a 2013 article on interfaith marriages, she argues the following:

> *It is high time to have the intellectual courage to tackle such topics while debating Islam to avoid the moral suffering and the feeling of guilt experienced today by many young Muslims, mainly, those who live in the West and are more likely to meet non-Muslim partners in their personal life.*
>
> *At the moment of choosing a partner, young Muslim men and women have to do it under their full responsibility with serenity, clarity and wisdom.*
>
> *Such debate is missing in our contemporary Muslim societies where unfamiliar ideas and the social conformism replaced the intellectual and spiritual honesty. Therefore, we should no more hide behind an unconvincing bastion of identity, but rather face the reality and admit that the world has deeply changed. We should also know that to preserve the spirituality of the heart, it would be necessary to override the hypocrisies and the social duplicity that eroded our current way of life.*
>
> *We should go back to the meaning, the purposes and the moral of the Qur'anic verse that talks about the interreligious marriage through a dispassionate debate that goes beyond emotions. We should review the real and deep meaning of some concepts in our globalized and multicultural societies such as 'the believing men and women' and 'People of the Book' … We should stress the main value and the initial spiritual trend that underlie this verse that calls for honesty, decency and the mutual respect as the pillars of any marriage.*[1]

Scholars and activists like Halima Krausen, Asma Lamrabet and Amina Wadud, among others, have served as important sources of inspiration in the 'making' of Mariam Mosque. What's more, I have identified ten contemporary Islamic scholars who approve of interfaith marriages. Around the world, such unions are increasingly being viewed as legitimate. They are already allowed in New York, Indonesia, France, Germany, London, Canada, Copenhagen and elsewhere. To my knowledge, Mariam Mosque is the first mosque in Scandinavia to perform interfaith marriages. We have had couples from Sweden, Norway and even France approach us in the hope of being able to get married. These couples have been rejected by numerous other mosques because the man happens to be Christian. It is my hope that, through this practice, we can demonstrate that the Quran takes gender equality into account and, as I argued above, this is the main source of legitimacy for interfaith marriages. But beyond this topic, the subject leads to other important questions, such as children's right to choose their own religion or the right of Muslim believers, both men and women, to fall in love with partners who are atheists or from other faith communities (including Buddhists, Hindus, Sikhs, etc.) that are not considered to be 'the People of the Book'. At Mariam Mosque, we believe that mutual respect within the couple is the most important aspect of any marriage. In order to be married at Mariam Mosque, a couple must first be married according to

Danish, Swedish or Norwegian law. We also seek the blessing of the two families. If that cannot be obtained, then we seek to negotiate with each family in order to celebrate an Islamic marriage in the best possible conditions. In late 2017, Tunisia was the first Muslim country to change its law and make it possible for Muslim women to marry non-Muslim men, a decision approved by a group of leading ulama in Tunisia. The decision has nonetheless created a debate in the Muslim world, but it could be the start of a new dawn.

CHAPTER NINE

Fighting Islamophobia

One man's imagined community is another man's political prison.

Arjun Appadurai

During the time of the foundation of Mariam Mosque, I sometimes had insomnia. I would also work until three or four a.m., asking myself a thousand questions. How can we create change without burning bridges? Why are some Muslims manipulating dichotomies between Islam and the West? Is it realistic to think we can lessen Islamophobia? If so, how? Can a group of women do it? Will we manage to change the negative image of Islam by writing new narratives with a focus on women's rights and the spiritual values of our religion? With these torments would come dark ideas about Islamophobia. I would think about the increase in hate crimes against Muslims in the aftermath of the terrorist attacks in Europe; about the young Muslim woman in London who was attacked with acid on her twenty-first birthday; about the stories of all the veiled women who have told me about the hostile glances they receive in public; about one of my dearest friends, Line, a Danish convert, whom I have known for fourteen years and whom I met through the Forum for Critical Muslims, when she told me that people spit on her in the street and treat her as a traitor because of her blue eyes and headscarf. I also ponder certain declarations that have been made by racist politicians.

When I have trouble getting to sleep, I tiptoe down the two flights of stairs separating me from the children's rooms. I go into the girls' room, then the boys', sitting down on their beds, watching and listening to the breathing of my little angels. After a time, I go back up to bed, having calmed down, and I go back to sleep. Even when you have a strong intellectual background and belong to a solid religious community, it's not always clear how to endure all the attacks we Muslims face on a daily basis. For children just starting out in life, for adolescents finding their identities, for refugees treated like second-class citizens and for all the other believers in vulnerable positions, Islamophobia is a difficult reality. So many millions of sincere, peaceful and welcoming Muslims are being unjustly accused. For nothing. Of course, I'm well aware that the problem is not on our side, but on that of the racists and Islamophobes. But I can't help feeling sadness and anger, though I am hopeful as well. This must change! Perceptions and mentalities must evolve. There's nothing impossible about this: I know the beauty of Islam, its wisdom, its appeal. It's probably difficult to understand for people who see the world only through the prism of televised news but, Islam is, at its core, a religion of peace. The name itself comes from the word *salaam*, 'peace' in Arabic. To be more precise, Islam is an active movement of people who practise peace by submitting to something greater than themselves. This isn't 'submission' in the negative sense of the word; Muslims simply admit that human beings are not the centre of everything, that there is something higher – just like Jews, Christians and Buddhists do among others.

Prejudice and anti-Islamic rhetoric are well rooted in the debate over Islam and Muslims in Europe, which is often based on threatening arguments. Such arguments are based on fear and other emotions, which often trump logical or humanistic forms of reasoning. I think back to a recent episode in the life of the Exit Circle, the secular NGO I founded in 2014 that takes care of women who have been victims of psychological violence. By the end of 2016, our growing network included forty volunteers and three local branches in Denmark's main cities (Copenhagen, the capital, Aarhus in the north and Odense in the south), but still did not have enough funding to tackle growing needs. A large social services NGO offered to make the association I set up a part of their umbrella organisation – but only on the condition that I leave my position as director! 'We can't hide the fact that your high profile, which is colourful and sometimes controversial, is a challenge for us', the potential purchasers respond. 'We'd prefer someone more neutral. Your double role as a religious leader and as the director of a secular NGO poses a problem. We would prefer a leader who was more neutral and less present in the media. Your title as an imam would put our chances of receiving funding from potential donors at risk.'

Still, it's strange: no one would be surprised to see a company director attending Catholic mass on Sunday or taking part in a Christian association. But when Muslims are in leadership positions, suspicion automatically arises. I'm the target of the 'soft Islamophobia' that pervades certain levels of society. For the board of directors, it doesn't matter that I know how to distinguish the religious from the secular, or that I'm *de facto* a Muslim secularist and just as at ease in Scandinavia as I am in the Arab–Muslim world. They also don't care about my multiple identities that make me many other things besides an imam, including a sociologist of religion, cognitive therapist, mother, activist and author. And they don't care that my Muslim profile has most likely been an advantage for the Exit Circle because it has helped us gain the trust of many women who otherwise wouldn't have dared knock on our doors. What matters to them is my religious identity: it obliterates all the rest. Is there not a contradiction in, on the one hand, demanding that Islam reform and modernise itself and, on the other, in not accepting the fact that Muslim leaders can direct social projects anchored in our society that are fighting the patriarchy? The answer is clear.

Along with this 'soft', almost 'friendly' form of daily intolerance come constant attacks from professional Islamophobes. At the beginning of 2017, when Aarhus, a large city in Denmark, was holding festivities for the 'European Capital of Culture' event, I was invited to give a talk at the cathedral. In this ecumenical and spiritual setting, I planned to centre my speech around the theme of 'The Value of a Community', drawing on my experiences as both the president of an association for abused women and an imam. But my presence in a cathedral didn't please everyone. A few hours before my talk, a Danish activist who became known several years ago for his scandalous actions (urinating on works of art, stripping naked and defecating in public places, all the while claiming to be subversive and intellectual) appeared outside the cathedral to organise a 'happening'. Accompanied by a cameraman filming his 'exploits', the performer went out that morning with a large wooden cross in his right hand, a Bible in his left and the firm intention of making a scene.

Stark naked other than wearing tennis shoes on his feet and a Danish flag tied at his neck like a cape, he entered the sacred place like a Viking or medieval pagan set on invoking fear. His 'artistic performance' consisted of reading the passage from the Gospel of Mark (11:17) describing Jesus's anger with the temple merchants in Jerusalem: 'Is it not written, "My house shall be called a house of prayer for all the nations"? But you have made it a den of robbers,' he declared in a stentorian voice. Having performed up and down the main aisle, he climbed on to a chair – still in his simple ensemble – and repeated the biblical passage. The 'artist's' message was clear: Aarhus Cathedral had to be purified by expelling 'the robbers', which was really a way of saying 'Muslims'. I was clearly being targeted. As soon as the performance was recorded, the video was posted on the internet, but to almost no effect. However, it left its mark on my twelve-year-old daughter Aisha, who had come with me to the cathedral and was looking forward to hearing her mother speak. In fact, we had gone into the church ahead of time and were almost the only ones there when he made his naked interruption. At that moment, I told Aisha to shut her eyes and, forcing myself to keep my composure, said in a calm, clear voice: 'He has the right to express himself, too, that's freedom of speech.'

Aisha replied: 'Why is he angry with you, Mother? I already told you to find a normal job. You upset people and it scares me – I don't want anything to happen to you'.

The artist's type of rhetoric finds a favourable echo among the members of the Danish People's Party. A few weeks before my arrival, several Danish priests and the far-right group's spokesman publicly criticised me: 'Sherin Khankan is going to preach in a Danish cathedral. This is an insult to the Church and to Christians who take their faith seriously. She doesn't belong to the Church! The Church's function is to preach the gospel, not Islam.' Of course, this politician was twisting the facts: at no point was either I or the organisers planning that I give a sermon or lead a Muslim prayer in the cathedral. I was forced to justify myself in the media: 'I'm not coming to preach as an imam; I'm coming to speak as an activist intending to share my experience in how organising an open-minded community can improve interfaith dialogue. Our different communities must not stigmatise each other; we must not exclude each other, but come together.'

A journalist from a daily tabloid interrogated me: 'All the same, do you understand that Danes are shocked by the mere fact that an imam is going to give a speech in a sacred Christian venue?'

My response was clear: 'No, I don't understand that. I've lived in Syria, where the Grand Mufti often invited priests to speak at the Great Mosque of Damascus. Interfaith dialogue that aims to speak to our points of convergence is not a new thing for me. Ecumenical meetings happen every day, all over the world. Why would they be impossible in Denmark?'

The debate around Islam has spiralled out of control. Muslims are being systematically criticised and stigmatised. It doesn't matter what they say or do. If they believe in Allah, then they have a problem. According to the Islamophobes, this must mean that they belong to a patriarchal religion that oppresses women. It's not important how they live out their faith: they are automatically guilty, liars, hypocrites. As stated

by a former representative from the Danish People's Party –
which, it should be noted, is the second-largest party in the
country – 'Muslims are only waiting until there are enough
of them to destroy us.' Following the same rhetoric, several
elected representatives from this party have, in the last few
years, been fined for 'inciting hate' after comparing Muslims
to Hitler ... and declaring that Muslim fathers regularly rape
their daughters!

Examples of insults or psychological injuries freely inflicted
on Muslims abound. More recently, posters sprouted up
around the country as part of an election campaign. This was
not long after the February 2015 shootings in Copenhagen at a
cultural centre and a synagogue (leaving three dead, including
the perpetrator). At the time, this slogan started to appear all
over Danish cities, in capital letters:

NEJ TIL
NAZI
ISLAM
ISME

(No to Nazi Islamism)

The formatting, in four lines, makes the words 'Nazi' and
'Islam' clearly stand out. Lumping them together in such a way
makes it easy to conflate the Third Reich with the religion of
the Prophet. And every day, honest Muslim citizens silently

walk by these posters, humiliated. At no point has it occurred to the minds of the posters' creators that the overwhelming majority of Muslims in Denmark are actually, like all other Danes, appalled by the attack on their country. The political party behind the campaign is Det Konservative Folkeparti (the Conservative People's Party). They do not belong to the far right, but rather the centre right, which shows that anti-Islamic rhetoric has permeated moderate political parties as well.

I could evoke a number of recent acts of hostility towards Muslims, such as the video that was posted in 2015 showing a Danish man burning a copy of the Quran (he later had to explain himself in court) or the recurring declarations of the leaders of the Nye Borgerlige (New Right) party – which appeared in 2016 and is even further right than the Danish People's Party – according to whom Islam is a threat to European countries and will never integrate into Europe. But I'll just ask a simple question: can you imagine a politician giving themselves permission to say that Judaism is a threat to the continent? And would people accept such a nationalist discourse that targets minorities? No, fortunately. However, in our country, the Islamophobes are well established. Some have even been elected to Parliament. They have unlimited coverage in the media, where they relentlessly pursue their dire objective: deepening the divisions between Muslims and non-Muslims.

In many respects, Islamophobia and anti-Islamic propaganda are the anti-Semitism of our time. Of course, these two forms of racism are not exactly identical, neither in their individual natures nor histories. But for Islamophobes, Islam is ontologically evil, dangerous in its very essence. Since 11 September 2001, the debate has been appropriated by reactionary forces relying on fear and emotions rather than knowledge, analysis and reasoning. 'Islam is violent, aggressive, threatening': this is the familiar tune that can be heard all over Denmark, and also in France, the Netherlands and the United States, through the voices of Marine and Jean-Marie Le Pen, Geert Wilders and Donald Trump – the modern-day Caligula who took the decision to proclaim a 'Muslim ban not long after inauguration'.[1]

After the attacks on the World Trade Centre in New York, the Quran became a bestseller and numerous pseudo intellectuals proclaimed themselves experts in the Arab–Muslim world. Yet the sacred text requires exegesis and an understanding of its context. But the Islamophobes – just like the radical Islamists – aren't worried about subtlety. On the contrary, theirs is a literal reading, without a historical perspective. Abstracting the context is the simplest way to manipulate *any* writing. It would be easy to take the Bible literally and come up with a fundamentalist – and anachronistic – reading of it. For example, Paul's first letter to the Corinthians (11:3–9) would be enough to claim that the biblical text is discriminatory towards women: 'But I want you to understand that the head of every man is Christ, the head of a wife is her husband, and the head of Christ is God' it reads. 'Every man who prays or prophesies with his head covered dishonours his head. But every wife who prays or prophesies with her head uncovered dishonours her head, since it is the same as if her head were shaven. For if a wife will not cover her head, then she should cut her hair short. But since it is disgraceful for a wife to cut off her hair or shave her head, let her cover her head. For a man ought not to cover his head, since he is the image and glory of God, but woman is the glory of man. For man was not made from woman, but woman from man. Neither was man created for woman, but woman for man.'

Or I could recite the famous 'sword verse' in the New Testament (Matthew 10:34) when Jesus says: 'Do not think that I have come to bring peace to the earth. I have not come to bring peace, but a sword.' If one were to read these verses literally and out of context, one could easily interpret Christianity as a warlike religion that oppresses women. My point is that one has to read the religious scriptures with references to history, theology and context. Christians in general do not read Paul's verses literally, or even take them into account any more. As for the 'sword verse', Jesus came with a revolutionary message, in which he intensifies and idealises the message of the Old Testament. At the time, following the new religion of Christianity was not an easy choice, and many followers had to leave their families behind. So, the 'sword' can be read as a metaphor for cutting family ties in order to follow Jesus. The same goes for the Prophet Muhammad. The message of Islam was not purely religious and spiritual; it was also a political criticism of the privileged Quraysh tribe, a defence of the poorest and weakest in society, and women's rights. Some verses have universal meanings, whereas others must be understood within their specific historical context and should be read as a universal message.

Exegesis plays an essential role in the understanding of all sacred texts. In the same way, 6 verses of the Quran, out of over 6,000, are susceptible to being interpreted as discriminatory against women: being a witness, polygamy, punishment (of women by men), inheritance, infidelity and concerning marriage. Discussions around the theme of gender do not date from today. The sacred texts are the object of multiple interpretations. The novelty comes from the fact that a new generation of women who have gained authority in the religious and intellectual spheres are challenging the patriarchal functioning of Islam and proposing a rereading of the Quran with regard to contemporary times. Among these women are Amina Wadud, Kecia Ali, Shaheen Sardar Ali, Asma Lamrabet and Fatima Mernissi. Shaheen Sardar Ali's remarkable doctoral thesis in law, *Gender and Human Rights in Islam and International Law: Equal before Allah, Unequal before*

Man (1998), shows how several verses of the Quran have been interpreted erroneously. In it, she argues that the few verses in the Quran that can be construed as discriminatory towards women can also be interpreted differently. In relying on Ali's work of reinterpretation, which greatly inspired and influenced me, I'm content to note six verses here that come up systematically in the media and in the comments made by politicians or commentators in order to depict Islam in a negative light, starting with the idea that our religion discriminates against women. In fact, a more astute analysis and an alternative interpretation of the text allows one to arrive at the opposite conclusion. In the following examples, I have been inspired by all the above-mentioned women scholars and by Shaheen Sardar Ali in particular, on whose work I have based my rereadings.

For example, verse 2:282 (from The Heifer Sura) stipulates that two people are always required as witnesses, and that in the absence of a man, he must be replaced by two women. Some have concluded from this that one man equals two women; yet in reality, only one of the two women in question functions as a witness and can have her testimony legally validated. The presence of the second woman can be explained by the necessity of her accompanying the first to help her in case she finds herself in a vulnerable situation with the other men present. The verse can thus be interpreted as a way of protecting the rights of women.

Another striking example concerns the highly sensitive topic of polygamy, in the sura titled 'Women' (4:3). Here, also, one must go back to the context of the time, which was full of wars and conflicts, causing a constant procession of widows and orphans. It is in a clannish perspective, with the idea of protecting widows and orphans in extreme social vulnerability, that this tendency to resort to multiple marriages must be understood. Again, this example has to do with protecting women who would otherwise suffer under a social stigma if they were alone and isolated, without a husband or socioeconomic security. Through remarriage, they regained rights and a form of protection, since the man at that time was economically responsible for the woman. In fact, the Quran explicitly states that a man can have only one wife except in cases of war. And it is advisable to listen to the serious exegetes of the Quran rather than the misinformed combatants of ISIS, according to whom a man can take several wives in order to satisfy his desires.

This is not to deny the troubling phenomenon of polygamy that has spread throughout certain countries (including Sudan and Nigeria) and which is also present on the margins of our Western societies. Unfortunately, some Muslims rely on the example of the Prophet, who had several wives, for justification. They forget that, with the exception of Aisha, his third wife, all of his wives were widows or divorcees. The main purpose of many of the Prophet's marriages was also to unite various tribes in order to create peace among them. And in any case, while polygamy can be understood in the medieval tribal context of the Middle East, it is unacceptable today – a reason why the marriage contracts written by Mariam Mosque forbid it; otherwise, the marriage contract is instantly annulled.

A third point of controversy concerns the idea that men are 'superior' to women and that a husband has the right to hit his wife in cases of serious marital disagreement. In fact, the Arabic word *qawwamuna* that appears in Sura 4:34 has several meanings and possible interpretations. It is often translated in the sense of 'to be above' or 'superior', but it could also be translated as 'to take care of', 'to protect' or 'to be a guardian to'. In the same way, the word *daraba*, translated as 'to hit' in some versions of the Quran, can also be understood as 'to distance oneself from' or 'to separate oneself from'. In no case does Islam recommend hitting anyone or getting angry. On the contrary, it advises that believers should control their annoyance and rage, as the Prophet does not approve of anger. In the new Danish translation of the Quran, the verb for 'to hit' (one's wife) has been replaced by 'to distance/ separate oneself from', and 'to be above' (one's wife) has been replaced by 'to take care of.' This changes everything.

The fourth example has to do with the notion of inheritance. The Quran (verses 4:7 and 4:11) stipulates that a woman's inheritance should be less than a man's. At the time of the Prophet, only the man was held responsible for the material comforts of the household, which is why this provision appears in the text. It does not have to do with any kind of sexism (a notion that was moreover unknown at the time), but rather a societal reality stemming from the ninth century. Even if the woman had money at her disposal, she was not held responsible for the family's material needs. In today's world, things have obviously changed. Men are no longer economically responsible for women. The deciding factor in this verse is that of family responsibility, not gender. So, if the man no longer has economic authority, this verse must be considered irrelevant. And, once again, we must not base the customs of the twenty-first century on those of the ninth. These verses, which correspond to a specific historical and social context, should be reinterpreted today. For marriages celebrated at Mariam Mosque, I instead emphasise the couple's shared responsibility. As a Muslim and a feminist, I am against the idea that social and family roles are determined by gender and that women must be in charge of domestic tasks. On the contrary, the husband and wife are partners who promise to help each other. If marriage were based on the principle that 100 per cent of the economic responsibility fell to the man of the house, just like in the Middle Ages, then many men would be incapable of getting married and starting a family, because their income alone would not be enough.

The one hundred lashes inflicted on adulterous couples (verse 24:2) is also an idea that has been spread by some ultraconservative Muslims, for example in Sudan, Saudi Arabia and Nigeria. As I've already said, according to the majority of Muslim scholars, this provision has no chance of being put into practice. First of all, some would argue that it actually requires the testimonies of four eyewitnesses. And it is enough to implore the name of Allah four times for the punishment to be annulled. What's more, according to the Quran, gossip is highly reprehensible. Once again, this is an example of a verse that must be interpreted metaphorically rather than a literal sense. I've also spoken of stoning: it is not part of the Quran, other than to evoke the repression that affected new converts to Islam, who were sometimes hunted down by their non-Muslim families and threatened to be stoned.

Finally, the sixth example has already been mentioned in the previous chapter of this book. It concerns Muslim men's right to marry non-Muslim women, whereas – again, according to the majority of Muslims – women cannot benefit from the same right. As we have seen, while the Quran doesn't recommend that a Muslim woman marry a non-Muslim, it also doesn't forbid them from marrying one of 'the People of the Book' (Jews and Christians) (verse 5:5). The Quran recommends that both men and women find partners who worship the One God and who are sincere and devoted to their faith.

Subject to interpretation, the Quran is what we call a 'dynamic' text, that is to say, it has its own life that evolves and adapts according to the time in which it is read. It is the object of unending debates, and must be placed in its historical, theological and contemporary context. A variety of viewpoints are expressed within Islam concerning how the Quranic recommendations must be interpreted and adapted to contemporary society, from a religious, political and social perspective. In this permanent negotiation, we women have an important role to play.

But Islamophobia is only one of two main fronts on which Muslims must mobilise themselves. The other side of the coin is terrorist attacks by violent groups calling themselves Muslims, which have struck Algiers, Baghdad, Bamako, Berlin, Brussels, Cairo, Copenhagen, Damascus, Istanbul, Lahore, London, Madrid, Mogadishu, Moscow, Mumbai, Nairobi, New York, Nice, Ouagadougou, Paris, Stockholm, Tehran, Tunis and many more. Since the end of the twentieth century, fanatics warring against the West and its values – as well as against Muslims – have been striking everywhere. These acts of terrorism are made by a minority of 'jihadists' or Islamists whose method is violence. The majority of Islamists in Europe and elsewhere, however, are non-violent and dream of a united Muslim world, which they call 'the Caliphate'. They are reformist or radical Islamists who have transformed Islam into a political ideology. They try to recruit young people through a simplistic understanding of the world. They lack the gentleness of our *ibadah* – our Islamic faith – and the deeper wisdom that goes hand in hand with the notion of pluralism, which is at the heart of Islam.

The Islamist party called Hizb ut-Tahrir is an example of an Islamist group in Denmark and elsewhere in Europe. They represent a challenge to European societies because they manipulate the dichotomy between Islam and the West and do not accept alternative interpretations of the Quran. They believe that their political interpretation of the Quran is the only one that is acceptable and valid, and therefore they see themselves as superior to other Muslims and all non-Muslims. I do not think it useful to condemn the party, but I believe that we should challenge the party members of Hizb ut-Tahrir with solid arguments, by establishing alternative Muslim organisations based on pluralism, and invite them to engage in critical dialogue. The critique has to come from within the Muslim community.

I can identify these young Islamists every time I give talks at a Danish university; they are there, for example, in Odense on the campus of the University of Southern Denmark. Not long after creating the Femimam movement – from where the idea for a women's mosque was born – these young men were present in the auditorium to hear one of my talks on Islamic feminism. At the end of my lecture, three or four of them came up to me at the foot of the stage. I always recognise their style immediately: well dressed in black suits, freshly shaved faces, between the ages of twenty and thirty. They work in small groups. They are rather arrogant and think they're scholarly, even though they haven't studied very much. They are often intelligent – intelligent enough, in any case, to manipulate a large number of less-educated followers – intensely obsessive and repeat their arguments in a loop. One of their first questions is: 'Hey, sister, where's your hijab?' Their tone is insistent but polite. It's a strange mix of aggressiveness and chilling courtesy.

I explain to them that I *am* wearing the hijab, but it's an inner hijab, representing sincerity and good actions. I also tell them that Muslim women have different interpretations of modesty and sincerity before God. Furthermore, I tell them that, according to the Quran, every Muslim – man or woman – must treat any strangers they meet with respect, even sometimes by lowering the eyes. 'What's your proof?' they demand, like police inspectors. They harden their stance. The discussion circles around the Quran and how it should be interpreted in a contemporary society. The subject of the 'caliphate' quickly comes to the table. Islam and democracy are incompatible, they argue. Better yet: 'Democracy is a threat to Islam.' They bring up the invasions of Iraq and Afghanistan and the situation in Syria, mentioning 'the crusade of infidels against Islam'.

I point out that the Islamophobia of certain politicians, Western hegemony or its occupation of part of the Muslim world (which I also condemn) doesn't disqualify the entire system. I ask them: 'What would you do if you managed to establish an Islamic state in the Middle East?' I add: 'Have you noticed that several members of Western democracies have gone to work in hospitals in Syria and Iraq to help save lives? And you, what concrete actions are you taking to help your fellow believers? Because, at the end of the day, it's our actions that define who we are.' Neither my questions nor my arguments seem to reach them. Unshakeable, they're immovable in their position. Insist on their arguments. Repeat their credo. Claim that Islam is superior to all other religions and that installing a caliphate would be to follow the natural course of history. While the majority of the students are long gone, I stay there for an hour. For these young men, the world is simple, divided between 'true Muslims' and *kuffar* (unbelievers). A frightening thought comes to my mind. Deep down, I think, their communication technique is hypermodern. Simplistic in the extreme, it makes a clean break with the past. They reason with slogans, focusing on their cause, repeating their arguments ten times, a hundred times, like populist propagandists. And, apparently, this works. Their words are perfectly adapted and calibrated for the age of social networking.

At first, I took the time to have discussions with these young men. I even argued for an hour. I would try to establish communication. However, I never worry about getting annoyed about divergent points of view. For one thing, I know that my main points are strong: I've mastered the content and meaning of the sacred texts. For another, I strongly believe in the virtues of contradictory and democratic debate. So, I always force myself to make my audiences sensitive to the infinite nuances of this religion of pluralism, especially when they are Islamists or Islamophobes. I express myself in a measured, nuanced manner, even to people who denigrate or threaten Muslims. I always make sure to act this way, in the media as well as in real life, because I'm conscious of the impact of my words, and I believe that adab (good manners) makes up half of our religion.

However, while I'm always careful when expressing myself in public (during televised debates, conferences, or talks at universities), I can be 'ruthless' and raise a detailed critique when I meet Islamists face to face in real life. Still, instead of demonising Islamists, it is better to counter them with solid arguments, because the way they manipulate dichotomies and thereby proclaim Islam as the one true religion is dangerous to any given society, including Muslim societies. To offer another example: at a university, a lecturer claimed that the notions of mercy and love were foreign to Islam, adding that they were present only in Christianity. I then explained to the audience the meaning of the names al-Rahman (the merciful) and al-Rahim (the compassionate) used for Allah. Both words come from the Arabic root 'r-h-m' connoting compassion, mercy, gentleness, source of all life and the womb. All the chapters in the Quran (except for Chapter 9) begin with the phrase 'Bismillah al-Rahman al-Rahim' (In the name of Allah the merciful and compassionate). According to the famous theologian, jurist and imam Ibn Qayyim al-Jawziyya (1292–1350), the concept of mercy (*al-Rahman*) is everywhere and includes all of creation, no matter how we behave or what we do, because we are all part of God's mercy. The name al-Rahim refers to God's mercy as a result to our good actions. If you do good to your fellow human beings, God will walk towards you. The point is that love and mercy are indeed a part of the Quranic message. God is merciful and shows mercy.

For me, the most effective way to fight ignorance is action. We must create viable alternatives to radical Islamist movements. The best way to deconstruct populism, whether it be Islamist or Islamophobic, is to 'do', to 'act', to 'build'. In a world where arguments don't matter (because people don't listen), concrete actions and activism are more effective. Our adversaries can easily dispute our words – but it's impossible for them to act as though what exists doesn't exist. It is irrefutable, for example, that Mariam Mosque opened its doors in 2016, that it brings together Muslim believers, that women imams run it, that they are called 'imams', that they take leadership roles in the mosque, that they give the *khutbah* and lead the prayer every Friday. No one can make those facts disappear. They are there. It's an established fact that women imams now belong to the same category in Scandinavian society as Lutheran pastors. Even the most conservative and traditional Muslims cannot ignore the fact that our elaborate model rests on a solid foundation of knowledge that legitimises us. Reciprocally, for Islamophobes, it becomes difficult to affirm that Muslim women are systematically oppressed based on the nature of the religion of the Prophet. With all due respect, it's now clear to all that we're taking our destiny into our own hands. This is the best defence against their backward and racist discourse. We've demonstrated that Muslims can change the narrative of Islam, challenge centuries of patriarchal structures, and assume spiritual leadership. And, evidently, the Islamophobes don't like that. New stories based on positive forces are taking shape. We are now walking in the footsteps of other movements around the world that have fought and are still fighting to challenge dominant discourses and practices within Islam that keep women from leading and thriving.

Before the Prophet Muhammad died, he gave a farewell sermon, known among Muslims as the famous *Khutbah al-Wida* 'Farewell Sermon', in his birth town of Mecca. The sermon summarises the core elements of the message of Islam: women are equal to men, black people are equal to white people, the poor shall be protected and have rights, charging interest is illegal, and the only thing that distinguishes one person from another is piety and good deeds. In sum: the road to Allah (God) is paved with good actions towards one's neighbours – women, men and children:

O People, lend me an attentive ear, for I know not whether after this year, I shall ever be amongst you again. Therefore, listen to what I am saying to you very carefully and take these words to those who could not be present here today.

O People, just as you regard this month, this day, this city as Sacred, so regard the life and property of every Muslim as a sacred trust. Return the goods entrusted to you to their rightful owners. Hurt no one so that no one may hurt you. Remember that you will indeed meet your Lord, and that He will indeed reckon your deeds. God has forbidden you to take usury [interest], therefore all interest obligation shall henceforth be waived. Your capital, however, is yours to keep. You will neither inflict nor suffer any inequity. God has judged that there shall be no interest, and that all the interest due to Al-Abbas ibn Abd'el Muttalib shall henceforth be waived.

Beware of Satan, for the safety of your religion. He has lost all hope that he will ever be able to lead you astray in big things, so beware of following him in small things.

O People, it is true that you have certain rights with regard to your women, but they also have rights over you. Remember that you have taken them as your wives only under a trust from God and with His permission. If they abide by your right then to them belongs the right to be fed and clothed in kindness. Do treat your women well and be kind to them for they are your partners and committed helpers. And it is your right that they do not make friends with any one of whom you do not approve, as well as never to be unchaste.

O People, listen to me in earnest, worship God, perform your five daily prayers, fast during the month of Ramadan, and offer Zakat. Perform Hajj if you have the means. All mankind is from Adam and Eve. An Arab has no superiority over a non-Arab, nor does a non-Arab have any superiority over an Arab; a white has no superiority over a black, nor does a black have any superiority over a white; [none have superiority over another] except by piety and good action. Learn that every Muslim is a brother to every Muslim and that the Muslims constitute one brotherhood. Nothing shall be legitimate to a Muslim which belongs to a fellow Muslim unless it was given freely and willingly. Do not, therefore, do injustice to yourselves.

Remember, one day you will appear before God and answer for your deeds. So beware, do not stray from the path of righteousness after I am gone. O People, no prophet or apostle will come after me, and no new faith will be born.

Reason well, therefore, O People, and understand words which I convey to you. I leave behind me two things, the Quran and my example, the Sunnah, and if you follow these you will never go astray.

All those who listen to me shall pass on my words to others and those to others again; and it may be that the last ones understand my words better than those who listen to me directly. Be my witness, O God, that I have conveyed your message to your people.

Thus the beloved Prophet completed his Final Sermon, and as he stood near the summit of Mount Arafat, the following revelation came to him: 'This day have I perfected your religion for you, completed My Grace upon you, and have chosen Islam for you as your religion ... ' (5:3).

CHAPTER TEN

Walking on the Sufi path

The perfect man is a woman.

Ibn Arabi (1165–1240)

I love Christmas. From October to January, our cities, villages, streets and houses are plunged into the darkness of the winter nights from the afternoon onwards. So families light candles in their windows, and these humble flames flickering everywhere transform the December darkness into a comforting warmth. I always go to the Christmas market in the fishing village of Dragør, five minutes' drive from my house, to buy my Christmas tree. It is a serious affair. I spend a long time choosing the tree that will be placed in our living room and I don't compromise on any of the essential elements. It must be six-and-a-half feet tall; the branches must be symmetrical, with no rebellious branches sticking out more on one side than the other; and the pine needles must be thick, still very green and with a strong scent.

Celebrating Christmas is normal for me because I grew up in a family that observed both the Christian and Muslim traditions: Christmas, Ramadan, Easter, Eid, etc. This gave us twice as many occasions to come together with family and friends. But once I got married, my husband, a Dane of Pakistani origin, saw things differently. 'Why do we need to have a Christmas tree if we're Muslim?' he asked, dead set on observing only the Islamic traditions and excluding all others. So the year I got married was my first Christmas without a tree. ...

This concession was really difficult because the Scandinavian traditions were always very important for my mother, and they mean a lot to me as well – they are a part of my identity, my childhood, my family memories. I can still see myself as a very young girl coming down the stairs into the living room in the early hours of the morning to look with wonder at our Christmas tree decorated with candles. My mother would be next to the tree, sitting in a chair reading or singing. This always gave me a deep sense of peace and belonging. In many ways, I associate the Christmas tree with my mother.

In Islam, Jesus is the prophet of love, and his name is mentioned several times in the Quran. Celebrating his birth and his life is perfectly compatible with being a Muslim. Fortunately, one Christmas, our oldest daughter Aisha, then aged four, jostled our family's new order with her childlike innocence –

and cunning. 'Baba, why don't we have a Christmas tree like everyone else?' she asked. 'Didn't Allah make nature and trees? So, if Allah made trees, that means we can have a tree in the house, like all the other children. We can just call it "the pine tree" rather than "the Christmas tree", if you want … ' And that's how the tree returned to our living room, though with a Muslim touch, because at the top of our tree, we put an Islamic crescent moon the children made rather than a shepherd's star. In many respects, the Christmas tree has become the metaphor of the Gordian knot of my marriage. My husband holds to a more literal and dogmatic reading of Islam, while I embrace a more inclusive reading, to the point of integrating elements from various traditions, including non-Muslim ones.

Among others, this anecdote sums up what the choice of the Sufi path signifies for me as a Muslim. I look for the deep meaning and essence of everything, behind each ritual and doctrine. And my practice is a quest towards unification: I seek to bring together differences and reconcile what people have separated through rigid doctrines. Sufism is defined as a spiritual approach to the Quran or Islamic mysticism. I am drawn to Sufism because I see it as a generous way of practising the religion. It is an expression of wisdom in which ethics, love, serving others, spiritual practices, *dhikr* (Islamic meditation), philosophy and asceticism, but also poetry, music and even dance, form a large part.

Even though it is not mentioned in the Quran or the Hadiths (the written record of the acts and words of Muhammad and his companions), Sufism is part of classical Muslim theology. However, opinions are divided over the origin of the name. According to one Islamic interpretation, Sufism (*tasawwuf*) comes from the word *safaa*, which means 'to clean your heart while uttering the name of God'; on the other, some Western scholars suggest that the word derives from the Arabic term *suuf* (wool) and refers to the ascetic life of people who wore long wool robes or caftans. But Sufism cannot be summed up in a single concept or definition. Across the ages and up to now, it has been defined and practised in various ways according to the different Sufi orders around the world. Some Sufis see the manifestation of God in everything. This open-mindedness leads to tolerance that in turn allows them to accept differences.

Sufism is not a denomination of Islam like Sunnism or Shiism. A person can be Sufi and Sunni – like I am – or Sufi and Shi'ite, or even Sufi and Alawite, etc. At Mariam Mosque, among the women who actively served the mosque in its first year, four women – all imams, khatibahs (those who give the sermon) or those in charge of Islamic spiritual care – are Sunni, whereas one of us is Shi'ite. In any case, no one pays attention to these differences. In Islam, Sufis have a particular function that relates to an interest in spirituality. While the ulama are the guardians of theology, and the fuqaha (jurists) devote themselves to the legal aspect of the religion through the study and interpretation of sharia law, Sufis are the specialists of spirituality, of the soul and the heart. Their vocation is not only to study Islamic rules and laws, they also seek to penetrate the secrets of wisdom by developing a methodology of the mind and heart and relying on it. The ulama, fuqaha and Sufis are all concerned with and involved in the science of each other, but they each focus on their own domain. In this regard, we can say that the first Sufi, before the word even existed, was in fact the Prophet Muhammad himself, who tells us: 'Die, before you die.' This means you must wake up to life by listening to your heart before it's too late and open up to spirituality in your life on earth. The spiritual approach to the Quran which, for some Sufis, implies an eclectic point of view, an openness to others and an 'opening of the heart', is what I call the essence of Islam.

The mystic poetess Rabi'a al-Adawiyya, who died in the year 801, is one of the first great figures of Sufism. Born in Basra, in what is now Iraq, she was the fourth child in her family, from where her name Rabi'a, which means 'fourth', comes from. According to one story, she was sold as a slave after her parents had died when she was still just a child, and only freed several years later as an adult. She never married and devoted her life to the service of Allah. Her exemplary behaviour, nearing saintliness, inspired her contemporaries, including several great wise men who followed her teachings.

I discovered her when I was twenty and was, of course, drawn to the fact that one of the first great figures of Sufism was a woman. Her poems define Sufism magnificently. One of them describes a scene in which several people meet Rabi'a as she is running with a lit oil lamp in one hand and a pot of water in the other. They say to her: 'O Lady of the next world, where are you going and what is the meaning of this?' She answers: 'I am going to light fire in Paradise and pour water on to Hell so that both veils (i.e. hindrances to the true vision of God) may completely disappear from the pilgrims and their purpose may be sure, and the servants of God may see Him, without any object of hope or motive of fear.'[1] Later, she expresses the idea of absolute humility: 'O my Lord, if I worship Thee from fear of Hell, burn me in Hell, and if I worship Thee from hope of Paradise, exclude me thence, but if I worship Thee for Thine own sake then withhold not from me Thine Eternal Beauty.'[2] God must not be worshipped in the hope of obtaining a reward.

With these words, Rabi'a al-Adawiyya handles paradoxes and deconstructs the most absolute of oppositions, that of Heaven and Hell, in order to bring about unification rather than division. The opposition between Heaven and Hell is well known. But dogmatic believers too often claim to be on the right path while in fact leading others astray. Rabi'a reminds us of one of the meanings of faith: we must strive not to love God out of self-interest, in the hope of gaining

Heaven and avoiding Hell; rather, we must believe in God absolutely out of a desire for Him instead of being concerned about our egos or expecting a reward. This type of spiritual love transcends the ego. Rabi'a reminds us that we must not play with dichotomies, whether concerning religion, cultures or peoples. We must seek now more than ever to reduce the oppositions between so-called 'good' and 'evil', Islam and Christianity, believers and atheists, modernity and tradition – indeed, between all the dichotomies existing in this world.

In order to experience divine love, each of us must stop wanting to monopolise God or connect God's image to our own interpretation; differences will always exist. But the point is not to concentrate on the differences that lead us to exclude each other. Sufism can be revolutionary in that it sometimes breaks norms and conventions. For me, Sufism is a journey within myself, over the course of which I discover the importance of knowing myself, as well as the spiritual dimension of the Quran. It is also a way to understand that the path to God is through our fellow human beings. When it comes down to it, Sufism is about serving others. You must know yourself to be a good servant. A man goes to the Prophet and asks him: 'How can I attain knowledge of the Truth?' And the Prophet responds: 'By knowing yourself.'[3]

Starting in the twelfth century, the philosophy of Sufi mysticism spread throughout the Middle East and Asia through various Sufi orders. The first Sufi group in Europe was founded in England in the eighteenth century. Over the next hundred years, it developed through literature, travels, commerce and the growing interest in the Middle East and Islam. In Denmark, Hans Christian Andersen, the celebrated storyteller but also keen traveller – including to the East – was the first Dane to describe the culture of the Turkish Sufis in his book *A Poet's Bazaar* (1842), in which he notably evokes the whirling dervishes of the Ottoman Empire. In 1925, Johannes Pedersen, a scholar who devoted his life to Semitic philology in Cairo and Copenhagen, was the first Dane to dedicate an entire book to Sufism. Around the same time, the Danish adventurer Knud Holmboe (1902–1931) converted to Islam after several trips to the Maghreb and the Middle East during the 1920s, and he describes his encounter with Sufism in Fez, Morocco – in which he participated in *dhikr*, the Sufi meditation ritual in which the participants sit in a circle – in his book *Ørkenen Brænder* (translated into English as *Desert Encounter*). Several Sufi orders mix meditation with social activism; they have thus spread all over the world in the form of social organisations and movements.

Sufism is characterised by the specific spiritual practice of Islamic meditation called *dhikr*. At Mariam Mosque, we practise *dhikr* once a month. We sit in a circle in the prayer hall where, for the occasion, men are welcome. During this mixed-gender meeting, we give ourselves a moment of silence to better connect with Allah, draw near to the Prophet and recall his life and teaching. At Mariam Mosque, Sufism takes a concrete form, as believers meet Allah by meditating, but also through the *khutbahs* (sermons) delivered during the Friday prayer, which are full of Sufi thought. Sufism is a practice for every moment. It is a daily application through which we question the meaning of our everyday actions and interactions with others, whether they be our children, or a stranger on the street or in a refugee camp. Faith surpasses the act of accomplishing the five daily prayers. Sufism is an ethical approach to human relationships and is based on forgiveness and mercy.

In the twelfth and thirteenth centuries, Ibn Arabi, whom I have already mentioned, arose as the great master of Sufism, which he defined as the religion of the heart. In an inspiring poem, Ibn Arabi proclaims: 'My heart can take on any form: / A meadow for gazelles, /A cloister for monks, / For the idols, sacred ground, Ka'ba for the circling pilgrim / The tables of the Torah / And the scrolls of the Quran. / My creed is love/ Wherever its caravan turns along the way / Love is my belief and my faith.' His message sums up one of the important ideas within Sufism. For Ibn Arabi, the heart takes a wide variety of forms and love manifests itself in multiple ways, without being limited to a single rigid interpretation. In Arabic, the word *aql*, for 'brain', also means 'to attach', 'to tie' or 'to restrict', whereas the word *qalb*, for 'heart' also means 'to transform'. Compared to the intellect, the heart has a much higher capacity for transformation. Ibn Arabi proposes developing a methodology of the heart and critiques rational discourse because, according to him, the Quran cannot be understood merely through rationality, as this approach quickly reaches a limit. When we seek to understand the Quran solely through rationality, then we run into paradoxes. One only need think of the Quranic story of Ibrahim who is ordered by God to sacrifice his son Ismail (the same story is present in the Old Testament, in which Abraham is ordered to sacrifice Isaac). God also tells him that his son Ismail will be the father of a great nation – the Muslims. God does not lie, and so both must be true. Though this is a true paradox for Ibrahim, he desires to follow God's will, and his heart is open and trustful. In the end, God sends an animal to be killed in Ismail's place.

For Ibn Arabi, it is unrealistic to circumscribe truth within a narrow definition. It is not up to humans to define the boundaries of religion, because we will never be able to comprehend the extent of Allah's power, forgiveness and mercy. We must abandon all grounds for judging others, since the journey to God starts only the moment the believer lets go and stops wanting to define the Divine. God is too big for us to ever fully encompass or comprehend, or much less define who God is.

I believe that Sufism, which is the way of love and the inner state of the heart, has much to offer our times, which can be marked by dogmatism, extremism, intolerance and the desire to monopolise the truth. Love is more revolutionary than hate, and Islam offers an anti-dogmatic way of thinking that Sufism can activate. Those who give in to the sirens of intolerance and call non-Muslims *kuffar* (unbelievers) deny the multiplicity God created. They are assuming a power that Allah has not given them and do not understand the extent of divine mercy. The religion of Allah cannot lead to hating and excluding others. God recognises Judaism and Christianity as the foundation of the Islamic religion. These religions, which precede Islam, are not a threat to Muslims. On the contrary, Islam is their prolongation. Denouncing other religions goes back to denouncing the source of all faiths and not recognising that Judaism and Christianity are the foundations of Islam.

The Sufi path can introduce nuances and offer an alternative to more conservative interpretations of Islam and to the Islamist positions that often tend to exclude people who think differently or deviate from their so-called 'True Islam'.

Come, come, whoever you are.
Wanderer, worshipper, lover of leaving.
It doesn't matter.
Ours is not a caravan of despair.
Come, even if you have broken your vow a hundred times.
Come, come yet again, come.

This famous text is often connected to Rumi (1207–1273), a Persian Sufi, mystic and poet born in what is now Afghanistan, who speaks to today's youth beyond the centuries that separate him from our time. Famous for his great works of love poetry, Rumi goes beyond the boundaries of Islam to inspire many people around the world through his writings and his openness to others. Like so many people, his non-dogmatic thinking greatly inspired me. When we invite Muslim believers to the Friday prayer at Mariam Mosque, we often quote Rumi so that people feel welcome, no matter their background. Lots of young Muslims feel excluded from mosques. I meet some who live in a difficult state of contradiction, because they yearn to be worthy of Islam, and so they don't dare cross the threshold of certain prayer rooms!

Some of these young people have grown up in strict or conservative families and have had experiences that have led them to lie to their parents and lead a double life with hidden romantic relationships. They feel torn between two worlds and are racked with guilt. As a result, some don't feel entitled to go to the mosque. At Mariam Mosque, we accept the fact that young people follow different paths. Some express feelings of guilt since they live different lives from their parents. But being a Muslim does not mean comparing yourself with the previous generation or with other believers who seem better because they stringently pray five times a day. Faith is not a competition; it is an endeavour of personal questioning concerning the deep meaning of one's own faith. The 'great jihad' (unlike the jihad depicted in the media) is the fight within oneself to control the ego. Sufism aims at humility, the essence of Islam. Its strength lies not in differences, oppositions or antagonisms. Opposition creates divisions, suspicion and fear.

Another difficulty for Muslim youths is the widespread notion, as claimed by right-wing politicians, that Islam is a violent religion. It's often said that Islamism is threatening Western democracies. As the number of Islamist organisations around the world, including in Europe, is growing, it is important to find a means to study or understand Islamist movements in a less dangerous way by introducing nuances. The idea that Islam is an all-encompassing ideology is not a marginal phenomenon. Islamist movements have become an integral part of the religion and society of the Muslim world, starting in the 1860s and continuing to this day. They were institutionalised in Egypt in 1928 with the establishment of the Muslim Brotherhood by Hassan al-Banna. The Brotherhood would later develop a new branch with Sayyid Qutb. In 1923, the first feminist organisations were formed in Egypt, followed by the Muslim Women's Association and the Muslim Sisterhood, the latter being directed by Laiba Ahmad and having its origins in the Muslim Brotherhood. Islamist movements are in part a reaction to the cultural encounter between the Muslim and European worlds, initiated by Napoleon's expedition to Egypt in 1798. Ever since this Napoleonic episode in the Middle East, Western predominance has long asserted itself. More specifically, Islamist movements can be understood as a critical backlash to secularism and Western domination. Some Islamists define 'Western values' as a singular whole in opposition to 'Muslim values'. For them, the rebirth of Islam is a reaction to Western secular influence.

Today, Islamism is multiform. To simplify things, let us emphasise its three main branches: reformist Islamism, radical Islamism and jihadism. The first, reformist Islamism, aims to change things from the bottom up by reforming the way people think, in order to reach an Islamised society, which is happening through the creation of political parties like Ennahda in Tunisia or Hizb ut-Tahrir in Europe and the Middle East. The second, radical Islamism, advocates revolution as a method to reverse the established order from above and to create an Islamic republic, like that of Iran. Finally, jihadist Islamists prescribe violence as a method of action. From this, it is clear that there are different forms of Islamist movements. Expressing these differences allows for the release of tension and the reduction of fear in public debate. All forms of Islamism are not the same, nor do they all encourage violence. As an aside, I don't like the term 'jihadist' because the true jihad, far from designating a holy war, implies the notion of the individual's inner struggle against their ego in order to conquer feelings of jealousy, envy and hate.

Islamism is a given in Western democracies. We must counter reformist and radical Islamist groups with rational arguments and offer an alternative discourse to their Manicheism that opposes Islam and the West. We also need to demystify Islamism, and Islamist groups need to demystify 'the West'. Our international debate on Islamism is based on a protectionist logic and arguments founded on fear. When people are excluded from societies, they often turn to alternative movements that can give them an identity and a sense of belonging; on the other hand, when people feel included in society, their way of thinking becomes more moderate. Inclusion promotes moderation. In my view, many young Europeans flirt with Islamism in their youth before leaving the ideology behind and moving on with their lives. People change. Instead of demonising young political Muslims, we should rather seek to understand why they feel attracted to such ideologies, counter them with rational arguments and offer solid alternatives. The Islamists' strategy of manipulating dichotomies is clearly threatening and damaging our societies and must be challenged.

Like the majority of Muslims around the world, I condemn terrorists and their violent methods. But we must admit that Islamism is a reality that represents a powerful and attractive force for a fraction of young people. In my opinion, the

Islamist parties seeking to transform political Islam are failing because they are using religion as an instrument of social control rather than as a vehicle for promoting social justice and equal rights. This way of approaching religion is problematic. However, my goal is not to condemn or pick fights, but simply to nuance the debate and propose something else to Muslim believers. Offering strong alternatives within the Muslim community is the surest way to fight radicalisation.

For us women, the struggle has begun, and it will be a long one. By creating the first mosque for women in Scandinavia, we have prepared the ground and opened up new possibilities. Other women long before us have opened mosques led by female imams, notably in China, the United States, Germany and South Africa. Now other women feel empowered enough to open more mosques for women. After ours, other houses of worship opened their doors in Berlin and will soon appear in Bradford, in the UK, and Norway. Mariam Mosque does not belong to a world movement or a global network. But, little by little, female imams around the world are connecting with each other, as well as with female rabbis and priests, along with leading scholars within Islam. Together, we are pursuing the same goal. Tomorrow – and even today – we are changing the way Islam is perceived around the world. Tomorrow, we will fight Islamophobia. Tomorrow, we will fight against the patriarchal structures within Islam and against interpretations of the Quran that allow for the discrimination of women. We will embody the peaceful and welcoming religion that is Islam by working the ground in order to change things from within. I will repeat our message tirelessly. Everywhere, from here to China. As long as ignorance is in power.

Since the opening of Mariam Mosque and through the process of institutionalising the Islamic feminism that went along with it, I have learned several lessons. The first is that things are built slowly, and on the basis of compromise. For a flower like this to grow, it must be rooted in tradition and community. Knowing one's own environment and being founded on a solid base are indispensable conditions for building bridges towards others. Changing things – and I mean changing them on a fundamental level – requires time, patience and humility. You have to give up the big ideas, the big ambitions and the big projects in order to move forward, step by step, and allow each person to keep up with developments, adapt to new things, take on new concepts.

At the beginning of this fight, I didn't want to burn bridges so I could remain a bridge builder and retain my alliances with traditionalists. But I soon realised that this was an illusion. Just by opening a mosque with female imams at the head, we have burned a lot of bridges. Burning bridges is a natural part of creating change. Revolutions are sometimes silent, at other times noisy. Ours situates itself between the two. I'm walking on a tightrope.

Already, a new generation of educated Muslims is gaining power through its own intellectual efforts, which are generating new stories in every field: the sciences, the arts, media, politics, literature. At the heart of this generation of 'new Muslims' are women who want to speak about their journeys, to share their stories. A new generation that, like the one that came before, wants to provide its own – informed – rereading of the Quran, one in which gender equality has a place. Sufism is at the origin of my feminist fight. It is my source of inspiration. And I believe that the Sufi path can advance women's rights within Islam.

Following this adventure, questioning patriarchal structures and opening a mosque managed and led by women has not been without consequences for me. Along the way, my private life has been impacted. People who were once close to me have distanced themselves. They cannot understand, or tolerate, the dynamics at work in such fundamental changes. I had to walk the path alone. I then realised, as I continue to realise to this day, in that reality, I wasn't alone, because God is the sustainer. 'The art of losing isn't hard to master; / so many things seem filled with the intent / to be lost that their loss is no disaster. / Lose something every day.' This could be a Sufi quotation, but it is in fact the words of the poet Elizabeth Bishop (1911–1979), which evoke the 'art of losing'. This is a universal theme for Sufis, called the art of abandoning oneself or the art of putting your trust in God. Breaking ties means letting go. It's setting yourself free. What will happen will happen.

If 'women are the future of Islam', as I've indicated in the title of this book, it's not in order to exclude men, but for the sake of finding a balance. We need men as much as we need women. Both must fight against patriarchal beliefs and practices. Fighting patriarchal structures within religious institutions, society and the family unit, independent of any religion, culture or social class, is one of the greatest challenges of our time. As Mariam Mosque has grown and developed, I've realised that another challenge, one that affects our young people, is the prohibition of interfaith marriages between Muslim women and Christian men. This situation is the cause of a great deal of pain, sorrow and conflict, both internal and external, for all young Muslims who have the 'misfortune' of falling in love with non-Muslims. If we are able to offer an Islamic response to this concrete, real question, then we can better serve our young people.

Mariam Mosque serves not only my own faith community but the larger community as well. I believe that European societies have a lot to gain by having access and exposure to a multidimensional Islam through a powerful, spiritually anchored mosque that preaches diversity, women's solidarity, progressive feminism, interfaith marriage and dialogue between female Jewish, Christian and Muslim spiritual leaders. In periods of crisis and division, we can share and come together as we did after the terrorist attacks in Copenhagen. Our aim is not to deconstruct Islamist, traditionalist or conservative positions, but rather to challenge these positions by strengthening contemporary women's place in the religious sphere.

In Denmark, the first female pastors were ordained in April 1948 within the Protestant Church. Today, the number of female and male pastors is about the same, and in the departments of theology at Danish universities, women have a higher representation than men. In my country, minority groups of Jewish and Muslim scholars, both men and women, are arguing for the same development within their respective religious communities by calling for full-time female rabbis and imams.

This change in discourse is challenging the established order. In any case, the fight must be taken up by both women and men, as well as young people of both genders. It must also involve more conservative and traditional imams in order to attain the spiritual change and modernisation we envision. On a concrete level, this could mean organising work meetings with them to freely discuss, for example, an Islamic marriage contract that gives women the right to divorce. By having a dialogue and exchanging our different points of view, we can advance and spread our ideas.

The fight for women's rights cannot blossom by remaining confined to women's movements. Progressive ideas about gender equality must enter male-dominated groups if we want to accomplish real change. The Arab Spring and other revolutionary movements in the Middle East were marked by the significant presence of women fighting for democracy. Women of all religions and political beliefs revolted alongside men to demand their rights. Today, women in the Middle East are fighting for a societal transition that will shift from patriarchal structures towards a democratic model. The goals of these women are connecting with the fight of women in the West.

The notion of patriarchal structures does not only concern the everyday dominance of men; it also affects abstract ideas and viewpoints, systems and structures created over thousands of years that impose certain patterns of control and power over so-called feminine virtues. Patriarchal structures are something that we disseminate, both consciously and unconsciously, to our children. Democracy doesn't protect us from patriarchal structures – they are within us, as we have interiorised them to various degrees, whether we are male, female or transgender.

Yes, women have always been an important part of the history of Islam. Today, they are claiming its future. Less than a year after the opening of Mariam Mosque, a man came to congratulate us. He was an imam. A great imam, from the Istiqlal Mosque in Jakarta, Indonesia, one of the top three most-visited mosques in the world, where around 200,000

Muslim believers go to the Friday prayer every week. He came and gave us his blessing, prayed, exchanged ideas and gave a speech. In his address, he evoked the words of the great Sufi master Ibn Arabi, from whom he cited a famous phrase: 'The perfect man is a woman.'

I would add that the perfect woman is a man. After all, Mariam Mosque and Islamic feminism are ultimately about going beyond gender.

Feminist rereadings of the Quran within Muslim communities have the potential to change the patriarchal structures and growing Islamophobia. Today such rereadings are reverberating in mosques, communities and families all over the world. Unavoidably, there are disagreements and conflict when women challenge male dominance; families are disrupted, marriages are dissolved. That is the price of change. I know, because that is the price I had to pay.

My sons play chess several times a week. I told them recently that the Danish word *skakmat* (checkmate) has Arabic and Persian derivations: *Shah mat* or *Sheikh mat*. It means 'the king is dead'. My oldest daughter Aisha laughed and said to her brothers: 'Watch out, brothers, the patriarch is dead. Long live the female imams.' She is right. Real change has to come from within Muslim communities. A new generation of Muslims is emerging, and awareness is growing that recognises gender equality as a basic and intrinsic pillar of the faith.

Notes

Chapter 1: The making of Mariam Mosque

1   An episode of World War II. During the winter of 1939–1940, the Finnish engaged in a tenacious resistance against a Soviet invasion. They stood up to the Red Army for 104 days.

2   The very same day Mariam Mosque opened, the French Conseil d'État, on a case submitted by the Human Rights League of France (LDH) and the Committee against Islamophobia in France (CCIF), stated it was against the 'anti-burkini' law in the commune of Villeneuve-Loubet (Alpes-Maritimes department).

Chapter 6: Looking at the future of Islam

1   Quoted in *American Muslim Women, Religious Authority and Activism: More Than a Prayer* by Juliane Hammer (Austin: University of Texas Press, 2013), 17.

2   Ibid, 20.

3   Ibid, 19.

4   Dr Jesper Petersen, whose research focuses on women imams in Europe, introduced me to the writings of Ibn Sa'd (784–845) in his work *Kvinderne i Medina – Imamer, Lærde og Krigere* (The Women of Medina: Imams, Scholars and Warriors).

5   Quoted in Ulrike Hummel's article 'Equality in the name of Islam', *Qantara*, 2014,

https://en.qantara.de/content/portrait-of-the-theologian-rabeya-muller-equality-in-the-name-of-islam

Chapter 8: Through earth, fire, air and water

1   Asma Lamrabet, 'What Does the Qur'an Say About the Interfaith Marriage?' 18 January 2013.
    http://www.asma-lamrabet.com/articles/what-does-the-qur-an-say-about-the-interfaith-marriage/

Chapter 9: Fighting Islamophobia

1   The presidential Executive Order 13769, titled 'Protecting the Nation from Foreign Terrorist Entry into the United States' and nicknamed the 'Muslim ban', is a decree signed by the President of the United States, Donald Trump, on 27 January 2017 (a week after he entered office) which suspended the entry of refugees and citizens from Iran, Iraq, Libya, Somalia, Sudan, Syria and the Yemen into the United States.

Chapter 10: Walking on the Sufi path

1   From *Rabi'a the Mystic and Her Fellow-Saints in Islam*, by Margaret Smith, pp. 98–99 (Cambridge University Press, 2010). See also the chapter on Rabi'a in *Women of Sufism, A Hidden Treasure: Writings and Stories of Mystic Poets, Scholars & Saints*, by Camilla Adams Helminski (Shambhala Publications, 2003).

2   Ibid., p. 30.

3   From *The Thoughtful Guide to Sufism* by Sheikh Fadhlalla Haeri (O Books, 2003).

Bibliography

Abaza, M. & Stauth, G., occidental reason, orientalism, islamic fundamentalism: a critique. In M. Albow & E. King (eds.), *Globalization, Knowledge and Society: Readings from international sociology*, SAGE, 1990.

Abd-Allah, Umar F., *The Islamic Struggle in Syria*, Mizan Publishers 1983.

Abu-Lughod, Lila, *Do Muslim Women Need Saving?* Harvard University Press, 2013.

Abu-Lughod, Lila, *Writing Women's Worlds: Bedouin Stories*, University of California Press, 1993.

Adams Helminski, Camille (ed.), *Women of Sufism, A Hidden Treasure: Writings and stories of Mystic poets, scholars and saints*, Shambhala Publications, 2003.

Ahmed, Leila, *Women and Gender in Islam: Historical roots of a modern debate*, Yale University Press, 1992.

Ahmed, Leila, *A Quiet Revolution: The veil's resurgence, from the Middle East to America*, Yale University Press, 2011.

Ali, A. Yusuf, *The Holy Qur'an: Text, translation and commentary*, Amana Publications, 1983.

Ali, Kecia, *Sexual Ethics & Islam: Feminist reflections on Quran, hadith, and jurisprudence*, Oneworld Publications, 2006.

Anderson, Benedict, *Imagined Communities*, Verso, 1991.

Arberry, A. J., *The Koran Interpreted: A translation*, Touchstone, 1955.

Badran, Margot, *Feminists, Islam and Nation*, Princeton University Press, 2009.

Badran, Margot, *Feminism in Islam: Secular and religious convergences*, Oneworld, 2009.

Badran, Margot & Cooke, Miriam (eds.), *Opening the Gates: A century of Arab feminist writing*, Virago, 1990.

Barakat, Halim, *The Arab World-Society: Culture and state*, University of California Press, 1993.

Beckford, James A., *Cult Controversies: The societal response to new religious movement*, Tavistock Publications, 1985.

Berger, Peter & Luckman, Thomas, *Den Samfundsskabte Virkelighed*, Lindhardt og Ringhof, 1987 (orig.: *The social construction of reality: A treatise in the sociology of knowledge*, Penguin, 1966).

Böttcher, Annabelle, *Syrische Religionspolitik unter Asad*, Arnold Bergstraesser Institut, Freiburg 1998.

Calhoun, Craig (ed.), *Social Theory and the Politics of Identity*, Blackwell, 1994.

Chittick, William C., *Sufi Path of Knowledge*, State University of New York Press, 1989.

Chodkiewicz, Michel (ed.), *Ibn Al Arabi: The Meccan revelations*, vols 1 & 2, Pir Press, 2005.

Clifford, James, *On Orientalism: The predicament of culture*, Harvard University Press, 1988.

Commins, David Dean, *Islamic Reform*, Oxford University Press, 1990.

Donohue, J. & Esposito, J., *Islam in Transition: Muslim Perspectives*, Oxford University Press, 1982.

Due Vroldby, Jens, *Den første velfærdsstat*, Frederiksberg, 1988.

Encyclopedia of Islam, vol. 10, Brill, 1956.

Esposito, John L., *Islam, The Straight Path*, Oxford University Press, 1994.

Esposito, John L. (ed.), *The Oxford Encyclopedia of the Modern Islamic World*, vols. 2, 4, Oxford University Press, 2001.

Foucault, Michel, *Discipline and Punish: The birth of the prison*, Penguin, 1977.

Foucault, Michel, *The subject and power*. In H. L. Dreyfus & P. Rabinow (eds), *Michel Foucault: Beyond structuralism and hermeneutics*, University of Chicago Press, 1983.

Gilroy, Paul, Diasporaen og identitetens omveje, In *Social kritik* (45–46), 1996.

Grøndahl, Malene, Rugberg Rasmussen, Torben & Sinclair, Kirstine, *Hizb ut-Tahrir i Danmark: Farlig fundamentalisme eller uskyldigt ungdomsoprør?* Aarhus Universitetsforlag, 2003.

Grünbaum, Ole, *Tusind og en nats samtaler: Fortællingen om digteren Rumi og vismanden Shams*, Tiderne Skifter, 2016.

Gülen, M. Fethullah, *Nogle begreber ved praksis af sufisme*, Kilden, 2004.

Haeri, Shaykh Fadhlalla, *The Journey of the Self*, HarperCollins, 1989.

Haeri, Shaykh Fadhlalla, *Prophetic Traditions in Islam: On the authority of the family of the Prophet*, Zahra Publications, 1999.

Haeri, Shaykh Fadhlalla, *The Thoughtful Guide to Sufism*, John Hunt Publishing, 2004.

Hjärpe, Jan, *Politisk islam*, Skeab, 1983.

Hourani, Albert, *Arabic Thought in the Liberal Age 1798–1939*, Cambridge University Press, 1983.

Ibn Arabi, *Sufis of Andalusia*, transl. with introd. and notes by R. W. J. Austin, University of California Press, 1971.

Ibn Arabi, *The Bezels of Wisdom*, transl. and introd. by R.W. J. Austin, Paulist Press, 1980.

Irwin, Robert, Writing about Islam and the Arabs. In *I & C* (formerly *Ideology & Consciousness*), (9), 1981.

Khankan, Sherin, *Islam & Forsoning: En offentlig sag*, Lindhardt & Ringhof, 2006.

Khankan, Sherin, A Muslim Manifesto. In *Politiken*, 2006.

Khankan, Sherin (ed.), *Muslimernes Islam: Religion kultur, samfund*, Pantheon, 2010.

Khankan, Sherin, *Paradis ligger under mors fødder: Barnets bog til muslimske forældre*, Haase & Søn, 2011.

Kuftaro, Sheikh Ahmad, *The Way of Truth*, Michael D. Berdine (ed.), University of Arizona, 1997.

Løgstrup, K. E., *Den etiske fordring*, Copenhagen, 1956, 2nd edn 1991.

Lorde, Audre, *The Master's Tools Will Never Dismantle the Master's House*, Penguin, 2018.

Louborg, Omar, *Sufierne*, Copenhagen, 1990.

Macleod, Arlene Elowe, *Accommodating Protest*, Columbia University Press, 1991.

Majid, Amér, *Sendebudet: Historien om profeten Muhammed og islam*, Gyldenhal, 2004.

Mansfield, Peter, *The Arabs*, Penguin, 1992.

Mehmood, Saba, *Politics of Piety*, Princeton University Press, 2004.

Mernissi, Fatima, *Beyond the Veil: Male-Female dynamics in modern Muslim society*, John Wiley & Sons, 1987.

Mernissi, Fatima, *Forgotten Queens of Islam*, University of Minnesota Press, 1990.

Mernissi, Fatima, *The Veil and the Male Elite: A feminist interpretation of women's rights in Islam*, Addison-Wesley Publishing Company, 1991.

Menon, Nivedita, *Seeing Like a Feminist*, Penguin India, 2012.

al-Murabit, Shaykh Abdalqadir, *The Hundred Steps*, Madinah Press, 1998.

an-Nabhani, Taqiuddin, *Thinking (at-tafkeer)*, Al-Khilafah Publications, 1973.

an-Nawawi, Imam, *The Complete Forty Hadith*, Ta-Ha Publishers,1998.

Pedersen, Johannes, *Muhammedansk mystik*. In: *Verdensreligionernes hovedværker*, vol. 10, 1952.

Petersen, Jesper, *Kvinderne i Medina, imamer: Lærde og krigere*, Magistrenes Forlag, Copenhagen, 2016.

Rabinow, Paul (ed.), *The Foucault Reader*, Penguin, 1984.

Rasmussen, Lene Kofoed, *Når sløret er et valg*, major thesis, Institut for Kulturociologi, Copenhagen, 1992.

Rasmussen, Lene Kofoed, *Den muslimske kvinde genfortalt: Nye narrativer i 1990'ernes kønsdebat i Cairo*, unpublished PhD thesis, Copenhagen, 1999.

Rauf, Imam Feisal Abdul, *What's Right with Islam is What's Right with America*, HarperCollins, 2005.

Roy, Olivier, *Skakmat: politisk islam: et alternativ for de muslimske samfund?*, Eirene, 1993.

Said, Edward W., *Orientalism*, Penguin, 1978.

Sardar Ali, Shaheen, *Gender and Human Rights in Islam and International Law: Equal before Allah, unequal before man?*, Kluwer Law International, 2002.

Sardar, Ziauddin, *Reading the Quran*, Hurst & Company, 2011.

Schimmel, Annemarie, *Mystical Dimensions of Islam*, University of North Carolina Press, 1975.

Sells, Michael A., *Mystical Languages of Unsaying*, University of Chicago Press, 1994.

Sharawi, Huda, *Harem Years: The memoirs of an Egyptian feminist*, The Feminist Press, City University of New York, 1987.

Simonsen, Jørgen Bæk, *Det retfærdige samfund: Om islam muslimer og etik*, Samleren, 2001.

Simonsen, Jørgen Bæk *Hvad er islam?*, Copenhagen Akademisk Forlag, 2006.

Skov, Leonora Christina (ed.), *De Røde Sko: Feminisme nu*, Tiderne Skifte, 2002.

Skovgaard Petersen, Jakob, *Sufibroderskabets Rituelle Liv i Religionshistorisk Belysning*, prize assignment at the University of Copenhagen, 1989.

Red.Skovgaard Petersen, Jakob (ed.), *The Introduction of the Printing Press in the Middle East: Culture and history*, (16), 1997.

Smith, Margaret, *Rabia the Mystic*, Islamic Book Foundation, Lahore, 1983.

Stenberg, Leif, Naqsbandîya in Damascus: Strategies to establish and strengthen the order in a changing society. In E. Özdalga (ed.), *Naqshbandis in Western and Central Asia: Change and continuity*, vol. 9, Swedish Research Institute in Istanbul, Curzon Press, 1999.

Stowasser, Barbara Freyer, *Women in the Quran, Traditions, And Interpretation*, Oxford University Press, 1994.

Terman, Rochelle, *Islamophobia, Feminism and the Politics of Critique*, SAGE, 2016.

Tønnsen, Aminah, *Islam: Koran, hadith, sharia*, Forlaget Mellemgaard, 2015.

Toor, Saadia, *How not to talk about muslim women*, In Steven Steidman et al (eds.) Introducing the New Sexuality Studies, Routledge, 2011.

Toor, Saadia, Imperialist Feminism Redux In *Dialectical Anthropology*, vol. 36. Springer, 2012.

Van Dam, Nicolaos, *The Struggle for Power in Syria*, I. B. Tauris, 1996.

Vasilaki, Rosa, *The Politics of Postsecular Feminism*, SAGE, 2016.

Wadud, Amina, *Inside the Gender Jihad: Women's reform in Islam*, Oneworld Publications, 2006.

Wadud, Amina, *Quran and Woman: Rereading the sacred text from a woman's perspective*, Oxford University Press, 1999.

Watt, W. *Montgomery, Muhammad: Prophet and Statesman*, Oxford University Press, 1964.

Wendell, Charles, *Five Tracts of Hasan Al-Banna*, University of California Press, 1978.

Acknowledgements

To my parents, Irja and Fayez Khankan, for balancing differences and standing firm next to me.

To my sister, Nathalie Khankan, for always being there.

To the father of my children, Imran D. S., for challenging my thoughts.

To my children for being patient, brave and loveable despite all changes.

To all the volunteers at Mariam Mosque for giving birth to a dream.

To the female imams, khatibahs and prayer leaders at Mariam Mosque.

To the men who stand beside the women at Mariam Mosque, Saer El-Jaichi and Hicham M.

To the female imams around the world for inspiring me.

To Jesper Petersen for his book *The women in Medina* and his support.

To Rasmus Alenius Boserup.

To Jacob Holdt, for sponsoring Mariam Mosque.